New Perspectives in Organizational Communication

Series Editors
Milton Mayfield, Texas A&M International University, Laredo, TX, USA
Jacqueline Mayfield, Texas A&M International University, Laredo, TX, USA

This series will examine current, emerging, and cutting edge approaches to organizational communication. Throughout this series, authors will present new ideas in – and methods for – conducting organizational communication research. The series will present a variety of topics, giving readers an in-depth understanding of the organizational communication field to develop the skills necessary to engage in field research.

Erika Darics · Jonathan Clifton

Organisation, Communication and Language

A Case Book of Methods for Analysing Workplace Text and Talk

palgrave
macmillan

Erika Darics
University of Groningen
Groningen, The Netherlands

Jonathan Clifton
Université Polytechnique
Hauts-de-France
Valenciennes, France

ISSN 2730-5333 ISSN 2730-5341 (electronic)
New Perspectives in Organizational Communication
ISBN 978-3-031-30198-8 ISBN 978-3-031-30199-5 (eBook)
https://doi.org/10.1007/978-3-031-30199-5

This Palgrave Macmillan imprint is published by the registered company Springer Nature Switzerland AG
The registered company address is: Gewerbestrasse 11, 6330 Cham, Switzerland

To my four boys: my biggest supporter, Imi, and our three sons who inspire my work to make the world a better place, one word at a time.

(Erika Darics)

To my family, in Belgium and the UK – the best ever – especially Tim (†) and David (†).

(Jonathan Clifton)

Acknowledgements

First of all, we would like to thank Jackie and Milton Mayfield, editors of the series *New Perspectives in Organizational Communication*, for giving us the opportunity to take part in this exciting project and for encouraging us throughout the writing process.

We also express our thanks to the staff at the hospice who allowed us to interview them and record their everyday workplace practices—warts and all! Although you have had to remain anonymous, we are very grateful for your time and patience.

We would like to express our gratitude to the Association for Business Communication, who supported this project financially through their small research grant and provided us with the opportunity to present parts of our developing work at various conferences.

We are also very much indebted to our colleagues around the world who, throughout the years, have inspired us and acted as sounding boards for the development of our ideas. Without this network of like-minded spirits, our research would never have left the ground.

Praise for *Organisation, Communication and Language*

"Darics and Clifton address the often taken for granted yet vital role of communication and language in the organizational sciences. Their approach gives particular attention to multiple communication methodologies to open wide an aperture on a broad range of challenges organizational leaders face. Their innovative application of communication method and theory advances organizational scholarship while simultaneously offering practitioners ideas to more effectively work through troublesome organizational dynamics."

—Edward H. Powell, *Leadership coach, Associate Professor of Management in the Graduate School of Business and Public Policy at the Naval Postgraduate School, Monterey, USA*

"A fascinating read, which makes the case for language awareness, based on an in-depth and multifaceted case study of a specific organisation. The authors have gathered enlightening data, and provide a hands-on approach to analysis and concrete takeaways for scholars and practitioners alike. I will definitely be recommending this to my students, both in management, and in language studies."

—Fiona Rosette-Crake, *Professor of English Linguistics in the Department of Applied Languages at Université Paris Nanterre, France*

"This is a highly readable, well-documented volume by two leading scholars in the field. It brings out the impact of the "small details" of language and demonstrates how they make organizations. The focus on method is very welcome: both students and more experienced scholars will benefit from it as they set out to do their own research."

—Geert Jacobs, *Professor of English Business Communication at the department of Linguistics at Ghent University, Belgium*

Contents

List of Tables

CHAPTER 1

Introducing Organisation, Communication, and Language and the Case Study Approach

Introduction

We live in an organisation society. From the local city council providing the infrastructure around us, to organisations that define our professional lives such as our workplaces or learned societies, to the organisations of our private lives—such as the sports clubs we belong to or the parent–teacher association at the children's elementary school, our local health centres, the supermarkets where we regularly shop—almost all aspects of our social and collective lives are related to, governed by, or deeply affected by organisations. We do not have to go far to find examples: a few days before writing this, a well-known, influential organisation—Facebook—went offline for a couple of hours. It made major news across the globe as its share price plummeted,[1] and the downtime had far-reaching knock-on effects on the lives of millions.[2]

Facebook is a good example to illustrate how complex organisations can be, and that their functioning and roles are not as straightforward as they perhaps used to be. Growing from a simple networking platform,

[1] https://www.thestreet.com/investing/facebook-and-instagram-whatsapp-reported-down.

[2] https://www.nytimes.com/2021/10/04/technology/facebook-down.html.

E. Darics and J. Clifton, *Organisation, Communication and Language*, New Perspectives in Organizational Communication,
https://doi.org/10.1007/978-3-031-30199-5_1

Facebook is now considered to be a major economic force[3] that enables millions of people to conduct and run their businesses. Yet, at the same time, it is considered to be a platform that threatens democracy (Marichal, 2012) through algorithms that determine the type of content people have access to, primarily through their private social circles.

The convergence of the once distinct boundaries between corporate, public, and private sectors, exemplified by Facebook, is becoming increasingly evident in various types of organisations. Public institutions, such as universities and non-profit organisations, are adopting more business-like practices and functions, emphasising efficiency and competitiveness. Conversely, business organisations are shifting their focus from solely pursuing profit to emphasising positive social and environmental impacts, aligning more with the traditional values of public and non-profit organisations.As organising and organisations become more complex and intertwined, they significantly influence our daily lives. The connection between individuals and organisations is bidirectional: we both shape and are shaped by these entities, whether in well-defined roles (e.g. as university lecturers, to use our own example) or in less explicitly defined but equally influential roles, such as a parent in a football club, a president of a parent–teacher association, or a member of a state where one adopts a new citizenship. By recognising the evolving nature of organisations and their increasing interconnectivity, we can better understand the intricate relationships between individuals, institutions, and broader society.For this reason, people aim to gain a better understanding of organisations and the extent of their impact on society and their personal lives. In social sciences, researchers have long studied the structure and management of organisations, how they learn and interact, and the way individuals within them work (Pugh & Hickson, 2007). Pugh and Hickson's (2007) concise summary showcases the variety of angles, approaches, and methods used in the study of organisations, highlighting the complexity of this field. And since organisations are complex and multifaceted, no wonder the starting points of research, the questions asked, and approaches taken by organisational scholars are "bewilderingly varied", as Rosemary Stewart so aptly describes (1997: 93).

To better understand this phenomenon, one can draw parallels between the study of organisations and the well-known fable of the

[3] https://www2.deloitte.com/uk/en/pages/technology-media-and-telecommunications/articles/the-global-economic-impact-of-facebook.html.

blind men and the elephant. In the fable, several blind men encounter an elephant for the first time and attempt to describe it by touching different parts of the animal. Each man, limited by his individual experience, describes the elephant in vastly different ways. The fable illustrates the difficulty of understanding a complex entity when only examining it from a single perspective. Stewart (1997) quotes an early publication of organisation theory (Haire, 1959: 2), who likens the study of organisations to this fable, stating that "there is little doubt here that it is a single elephant being discussed, but, by and large each of the observers begins the description from a different point, and often with a special end in view".

Considering that the study of organisations has evidently been so varied—and perhaps even disjointed—readers may wonder whether there is a need, or even a space, for a new angle in organisational research at all. We believe there is, and a simple one at that: language.

Of course, the idea of exploring organisations through a language lens is not new by any means: it has been around since what is known as the "linguistic turn" in organisational research, explained in Alvesson and Kärreman's (2000) oft-cited essay, but has its roots in a much earlier linguistic turn in analytic philosophy (Hacker, 2013). We also need to emphasise that we are not alone in our belief, as the burgeoning field of organisational discourse, and the breadth of work we quote in this book, demonstrate. But accepting its centrality and being able to scientifically examine language are two distinct issues, and this is where our book aims to make a contribution. The main purpose of this book is to make visible, tangible, and actionable the link between language and organisational realities. By making such a link between concepts, we also hope to connect two camps: scholars who make the mechanics and small details of language their object of scientific inquiry and scientists who focus their attention on exploring organisational realities. For the latter group, the book aims to show how to explore organisational phenomena (such as *organisational sense-making* in Chapters 3 and 4, *leadership* in Chapter 5, *organisational identity* in Chapter 6, *team spirit* in Chapter 7, *sociomateriality* in Chapter 8, and *organisational healing* in Chapter 9) through a language lens. For linguists and discourse scholars, we aim to demonstrate how analytical methods familiar to them (such as metaphor analysis, narrative analysis, membership categorisation analysis, conversation analysis, interactional sociolinguistics, or metadiscourse analysis) can be used not only to explore but also to explain various aspects of social reality in organisational life. The main mission of this book is to strengthen (or, where needed, to build) bridges between linguistic research and organisation theory.

A Close(r) Look at Language

To make our case for the close examination of language, we would like to introduce another elephant, the one "in the room" (i.e. a controversial and obvious issue that people are aware of but which they ignore). In this context, the elephant represents the often overlooked yet critical issue of language. The centrality of language is acknowledged in many schools of academic scholarship, where the basic premise is that language constitutes our social reality. This perspective broadly suggests that "internal cognitive processes are no longer conceptualised as the origin of meaning. Instead, meaning is actively produced, reproduced, negotiated, and maintained in social interaction" (Jian et al., 2008: 302). Simply put, we talk (or write) our realities into being, especially when it concerns realities, such as hierarchy, power, gender, trust, threat, and success—just to name a few. Organisations are a good example of this constitution. As Mautner (2017: 611) notes,

> every step in the life of an organization, from its foundation to the moment when it is wound up, is a discursive act of some sort … Day-to-day activities in organizations are either accompanied by texts and interaction or consist entirely of them. Interviews, meetings, and reports, for example, as well as the archetypal "watercooler chat", are just a few of the myriad genres without which organizations simply could not function.

Organisational discourse research argues that communication is the very substance through which organisations come to exist (for more on this, see Chapter 8). Researchers who view communication as constitutive of social and organisational realities, or the "stuff of organizing" as organisational communication scholars Putnam and Mumby (2014: 3) express it, propose that organisational phenomena can be better understood by observing and analysing communication processes. As Putnam and Mumby (2014: 4) further explain, this approach "adds something unique and significant to the body of knowledge about people and their organizational lives".

In this book, we aim to illustrate the extent to which we can learn about organisations, their processes, and the people within them by concentrating on communication. We will achieve this by delving into micro-level detail and examining the linguistic and communicative practices of organisational members. This focus stems from the rationale that if communication forms the basis of organisations, then language (alongside other meaning-making resources) serves as the fundamental building blocks for this construction. By investigating how language functions, we can gain a more nuanced understanding of communication and, consequently, organisational phenomena, thus emphasising the importance of examining small linguistic details within broader social contexts.

Let us give an example. In a research study, Kirby and Krone (2002) interviewed employees to talk about their experiences concerning how work–life balance policies are implemented and understood in their organisation. The authors noticed a pattern in the employees' responses. For example, stories about how the use of such policies created more work for the others, or that women were thought—and expected—to be the greatest beneficiaries of these policies, were commonplace. These "ways of talking" and the ways in which organisational players perceived the legitimacy and reason to use them had a considerable effect on how well these policies were utilised. So what employees said, and *how* they talked, about work–life balance policies provided a window both into what they thought about work–family policies and wider organisational and societal expectations about gender roles, work–life balance, and orientations of individualism. The "unique and significant" lesson from this observation was that despite the availability and access to several family-friendly policies, how these were taken up was influenced by how colleagues talked about them.

So, if language—how we talk and write—has such importance, it seems to be a logical next step to take a close look at it. Just how close we look matters, though: Are we poking our elephant with a long stick from across the room or do we walk up close to examine the finest details of its skin? The answer to this question of course lies in how researchers are trained. As far as communication is concerned, those of us trained to observe and examine the mechanics and details of language use tend to look very closely. This means an interest in the smallest detail of linguistic production: if the reader is intrigued, perhaps it is a good time to have a cursory look at the excerpt analyses throughout the book. When we say small detail, we *do* mean small detail, ranging from the choice of words (Chapter 3), sequences of turns at talk (Chapter 8), to pronoun use (Chapters 5 and 6).

This close look at the details of language use is not always self-evident, however. As Mautner (2016: 21) observes, research concerned with organisational discourse "appears to err on the side of *macro* … concerns, with little eye for detailed linguistic mechanisms". In her critique she highlights that "textual analysis often begins and ends with *fairly coarse content analysis* even though … one and the same content can be expressed in myriad ways by subtly tweaking linguistic devices" (Mautner, 2016: 21, italics added). This book makes a case for, and importantly demonstrates, how such "macro" or "coarse" approaches can be successfully complemented by findings about the minutiae of language use—the micro.

Of course, this does not imply that language has been disregarded by scholars interested in organisational realities. Putnam and Fairhurst (2001: 78) celebrated the emergence of language analysis as it began to occupy "a prominent place in organizational studies". Several years later, however, literature reviews of language-focused management and organisational research (see, e.g., Lockwood et al., 2019; Murphy & O'Brien, 2006) suggest that language analysis has not become as prominent, precise, or systematic as one might have anticipated given the initial enthusiasm.

This issue brings us back to the analogy of the blind men and the elephant. In the fable, the main characters explored certain parts of the elephant, ultimately failing to grasp the whole picture. In research, many scholars examine language from a distance, focusing on macro structures, frames, or grand narratives. They do so "mostly in isolation, overlooking the construction and consequences of potential assemblages of multiple linguistic strategies" (Lockwood et al., 2019: 27). The pitfall of such an approach is of course that if we examine the role of language and communication within organisations and the process of organising based solely on broad concepts, we are prone to overlook the minute details that, on the one hand, show *how* language constructs organisational reality and, on the other, *how* social realities, ideologies, or shared understandings impact language and communication. Echoing the criticism, referred to above, that Mautner (2016) made, these authors also advocate a deeper understanding of how actual linguistic practices occur, increased attention to language in interaction, and examination of how language constitutes or contributes to various social realities in organisations. It is this call that our book aims to address.

The Role of Text and Talk

So far in our introduction we have explored the significant role that organisations play in our daily lives, and we have highlighted the crucial function language serves as a constitutive force that "talks organisations into being". However, the most prevalent view people may have about communication, particularly in the context of work, is typically not the constitutive role we explained above. Communication, and by extension language, is often understood as a technical skill utilised to achieve professional goals. The pursuit of mastering *effective communication* has become a lucrative industry, evident in the burgeoning number of publications, internet help sites, and workplace training programmes. The prevailing perspective remains highly instrumentalist, treating language and communication as mere means to an end. This view appears to overlook the constitutive role we discussed above. This blind spot may stem from two issues: first, the instrumentalist view that language is a functional "tool", where the use of certain linguistic elements will inevitably lead to pre-defined, predictable effects, and second, the view of language as a neutral "mirror", with the help of which we can objectively describe or depict reality. Below, we explore these in greater detail.

From an instrumentalist perspective, communication is seen as a tool for achieving personal goals and conveying information. Consequently, linguistic skills are considered to be part of a technical skill set. This view suggests a direct correlation between a communicator's intentions, the strategies used, and the outcomes achieved (Darics, 2019). The understanding of communication as merely a technical skill was evident in the early phases of the consultancy project this book is about. When we joined the organisation—a local hospice which provides crucial end-of-life care for patients in their own home, at an inpatient ward, and a day centre—as part of a consultancy project, the original goal was to improve the communicative effectiveness of the fundraising team. The hospice's work is partially funded by the government, but the majority of their funding is—or rather should be—raised from donations from the wider public. Even though the brief for the consultancy specified a focus on team effectiveness, when we interviewed group members about what they would like to get out of this project, without exception they all said something relating to their own communication skills, for instance, issues with being too direct or establishing better channels of communication with other teams. These responses seemed to reinforce the team's understanding that a communication consultancy helps the team members improve their communication practice. That said, there was some acknowledgement of the various complex aspects of communication; in fact, Kira, one of the team members, said the following:

Extract 1.1

Kira I'll be quite interested to see the difference in how I speak with different
people (0.5) it'll be be quite interesting as I think I probably speak
differently with people who I feel they're giving us something and we're
giving them something and there's other cases where they're just giving us
something we've got to be very thankful you know

In Extract 1.1, Kira expresses an interest in observing the differences in her communication style when interacting with different people. She acknowledges it is important to vary her communication depending on the relationship with her interlocutor and the intended outcome of the interaction. The idea of being able to employ different linguistic strategies to achieve specific goals is telling of her understanding of communication as a technical skill. However, we need to note that even though the instrumental conceptualisation is to some extent "right", it is not exclusive: language always has a constitutive function too. In Kira's case, for example, her choice of words and style not only serves as a tool to achieve her objectives but also contributes to how she constructs the idea of her team as opposed to donors and other volunteers (see also Chapter 7). Similarly, her linguistic choices reflect the organisational identity and values she represents, and, through her corporate messaging, Kira influences perceptions of her organisation, shaping how others view its identity and values (more on this in Chapter 6). Thus, we can see that while the instrumentalist view of communication is valid, it does not exist in separation from the constitutive role.

The second source of confusion is the assumption that language is an objective mirror of reality, one that exists independently of human interpretation. Instead, as we have already discussed above and will argue in what follows, language should be viewed as dynamic and a contextually bound social practice that constructs social reality through interactions. This view of language has been influential in various fields of organisational research since the so-called linguistic turn in the late twentieth century (Alvesson & Kärreman, 2000; Chia, 2000). Despite the growing recognition of the role of language in shaping social reality, this view needs to be more widely acknowledged among scholars, educators, and practitioners.

Musson, Cohen, and Tietze have repeatedly highlighted that the centrality of language in organisational processes, with a few exceptions, is not appropriately addressed in management curricula. They argue that management education that denies students discursive consciousness perpetuates the theory/practice divide that is so typical of the field (Cohen et al., 2005; Musson et al., 2003, 2007). The problem is that the importance of language in organisational life is often taken for granted and rarely considered in its full complexity. Language is so fundamental to organisational life that it is often overlooked, with little consideration given to what it involves or how important it is to our understanding of organisations. This book sets out to change this perception, and to demonstrate not just why it is timely and important to incorporate a deeper understanding of language in organisational research and education but also to show how this knowledge can bridge the gap between theory and practice and better prepare us for the complexities of organisational life.

The Case Study

This book is based on a single case of the fundraising team who we worked with as communication consultants following a restructuring exercise. Generally speaking, because cases offer insight into organisational processes in their natural contexts, scholars have long used case studies for exploring and understanding complex phenomena. As Dyer and Wilkins (1991: 614) argue, the careful study of a single case has frequently led scholars "to see new theoretical relationships and question old ones", in part because such focused research permits "the deep understanding" of an entity. The case study approach is highly qualitative, though—which means that it does not lend itself to generalisations based on statistical significance. This is an argument quantitative researchers often use. But dismissing case-based research because of such an argument would mean missing out on what Gummesson (2017: 159) calls *analytic generalisation*: discovering the patterns that exist instead of investigating how often or to what extent (more on this in Chapter 2). Dyer and Wilkins (1991: 614) suggest that *better stories, not better constructs, generate better theory*—and in this book we have taken this suggestion to heart. We use the story of an income generation team running through the chapters of this book to explore various concepts of organisational life such as change management and leadership. Working with key members of the team allowed us to gain a deep insight into their everyday organisational realities and working practices—these are the insights we will share with the readers throughout the book.

Case studies can be intrinsic, instrumental, and collective (Stake, 1995). Intrinsic case studies focus on a single case that is worthy of analysis because it is interesting or unique in itself. Such work aims to develop an understanding of the processes, causes, and effects in one distinguishable event. Our fundraising team would be worthy of such attention, especially in light of the outcome of the consultancy itself, which concluded that many of the problems that became evident were the result of badly managed change processes (see more on this in Darics, 2020). Our story, however, is a classic example of what Stake (1995) calls an *instrumental* case: we use our data both to illustrate the points we make about broader organisational phenomena and to "showcase" the application of language-centred analytical methodologies. For this reason, we draw on different types of data when they best illustrate, explain, and showcase, ranging from interviews conducted with key team members, to recordings of talk, to digital and corporate communication data.

The Team

The consultancy took place in a hospice located in a close-knit community in the UK. The primary function of the hospice is to deliver comprehensive end-of-life care services, including emotional and spiritual support, and assistance to patients' families in coping with grief and loss. It was founded in the late seventies and grew from a small palliative care unit to a hospice with a day centre with nearly 20 bedrooms and an outpatient unit. Throughout the year, the hospice also provides educational programmes and carries out fundraising activities that play a key role in the life of the community. The hospice's operational costs are only partially funded by the government (30%), thus making it necessary for the hospice itself to raise the missing 70%, approximately £7 million annually, to maintain and enhance its services. This financial goal is achieved through the concerted efforts of the income generation team—who will take centre stage of the case study. This team plays a pivotal role in the hospice's financial stability. This is because they are responsible for developing and executing fundraising strategies to engage potential donors and secure vital funding. The team organises various fundraising events and drives, and represents the hospice at local events not only to raise funds but also to heighten community awareness of the hospice's mission and services. Volunteers are an important part of the team, and the core members collaborate closely with them to organise and execute fundraising events and other initiatives. In this case study, however, we are going to focus on the core paid members of the team. Before we introduce them, though, it is important to talk about the recent restructuring that took place in the hospice, which had a fundamental effect on the makeup and members of the team.

Just before the consultancy took place, the hospice underwent a significant restructuring process. They took advice from a national umbrella organisation so that they could adapt to the newly introduced funding environment of the UK. The aim of the restructuring process was to "place the right people in the right jobs" (as we learnt from one of our interviewees, Dot) and to ensure that the hospice would be able to continue operating effectively. However, the implementation of the changes faced some challenges and the hospice sought advice from an external HR company, one which lacked knowledge of the local context and the hospice itself. The HR company proposed a categorisation system to rank positions from one to four, with one being the safest position and four indicating that the job no longer existed. This ranking exercise created a lot of anxiety for existing employees and even led to voluntary and involuntary redundancies (we have written about one such case previously in Darics and Clifton [2019]). This is the context in which we got to meet the team, and this team was led by Amy. An established fundraising consultant with years of experience, Amy joined the team following the restructuring and had been in place for 11 weeks when we met her. As a strong leader, she implemented a flat structure where everyone reported directly to her. Throughout the book, we will explore her leadership style based on motivation and close communication.

Dorothy, or Dot as she was known, was the longest-serving team member with five years of experience as an events organiser. Since she had had to experience it first-hand she found the restructuring process traumatic. Nonetheless, she respected Amy and appreciated the team's new structure. Having completed a "Leading from the Middle" course, Dot valued stronger connections within the hospice and with volunteers and saw herself as a key contact point for those returning to volunteering post-restructuring.

Kira was a 28-year-old with a management degree. She had been with the hospice for nine months. She initially served as interim head during the restructuring, which, according to other team members, was just as big a surprise for her as for others. Her role involved liaising with major donors and corporations, organising events, and communicating with the press and local organisers. In Chapter 3, we will hear about her transition back to an assistant role after Amy's arrival.

Rick had been a database assistant for three years. Originally moved over from the finance department, he interacted with the fundraising team and reported to Amy. His responsibilities included creating posters, maintaining the website, and managing the database to ensure accurate records and communication.

Kit was the youngest team member and referred to herself as being "at the bottom of the food chain". As an events assistant alongside Kira and Dot, she had the least responsibility. Having joined the hospice nine months before the consultancy, she experienced the aftermath of the restructuring and had to figure out her role independently before Amy's arrival. Kit's tasks included managing emails, social media, and other communications, drawing on her university studies in social media management.

As the reader can see, the team was relatively "young", Dot being the only member who stayed over from the fundraising team in the previous structure. This may be why their sense of being a team had just recently developed, as Dot explains in her interview:

Extract 1.2

1	Dot	we work very much together an = and Amy saw that straightaway so she's
2		actually put us all = all of us report to Amy so none of us err go through each
3		other so we've become much more of a team euh (.) but that's only really
4		recently (.) literally weeks this is perfect timing

The Research and the Consultancy

The timing of the consultancy at the hospice was described as perfect by Dot (Extract 1.2), yet its occurrence was not incidental. Amy initiated it, inviting us to observe and work with the team to improve their communication and efficiency as fundraisers. We agreed to provide our help as volunteers on the condition that we could use the data collected beyond the consultancy for academic research. However, balancing practical problem-solving with academic research presented challenges that we, as consultant researchers, encountered.

Time emerged as a critical issue during the consultancy. The organisation required immediate solutions, preventing us from completing a thorough and systematic analysis of all the data at the time of the consultation. Academic research, on the other hand, requires a longer-term perspective, including sufficient time to embed the analysis in the context of established lines of research, as well as conducting, discussing, and making sense of the findings both within the context of the consultancy and in the broader context of academic scholarship. The very publication of this book years after the actual consultancy is a case in point about the tension between the two timeframes.

Another point of tension that emerged during our consultancy was the critical aspect of our research. Academic research is driven by contributing to social good, but when research is governed by practical issues—and even by the agenda of the clients—maintaining neutrality and critical distance becomes a hard exercise. In our consultancy work providing a critical angle was challenging, particularly because our research challenged top-down decision-making and power imbalances within the organisation. As we have written elsewhere, such a critical approach can jeopardise the success of the consultancy, especially if research "conducted in the ethos of academic scholarship is thought to affect ... the pride of those involved" (Darics, 2020: 58).

In terms of our presence and role, readers may have noticed that above we referred to ourselves both as researcher consultants and as consultant researchers. We think this is an important distinction, not least because our role and identity shifted throughout our days of data collection. In ethnographic research, researcher positionality has been extensively problematised because the various roles researchers adopt can range from "neutral" observer to active participant, and as Vallaster (2000: 474) notes, a lot depends on the researcher's intuition and flexibility to balance his or her "formal vs informal" or "private vs professional" role within the different contexts. In corporate contexts, these dichotomies can be further expanded, and researchers can be ascribed different identities by the organisational members. For example, if the researcher gains the trust of interviewees who open up about a topic that they would not normally discuss with other team members or the management, as Lønsmann (2016) found, the researcher is ascribed the identity of the "confidant". This was certainly the case in our consultancy, as the interview extracts in Chapter 3 and our earlier study (Darics & Clifton, 2019) attest. We were also ascribed the identity of "communication expert": above, we have quoted Kira who expected us to feedback on her communication style, and we heard similar requests from all core members we worked with. The important realisation that resulted from the acceptance of our shifting positionality and the identities that were ascribed to us is that these inevitably affected the data we collected. These ascriptions of identity may have influenced what organisational members said and what information we gained access to (see also Lønsmann, 2016). And access, as we will see in the next chapter, is fundamental to obtaining the data necessary for the fine-grained analysis that we advocate in this book.

Concluding Remarks

In this chapter, we introduced the theoretical foundations of our work, emphasising the role of language in shaping organisational processes and outcomes. We have challenged the popular assumption that language merely serves as a "soft skill" or an objective mirror of reality, and instead emphasised the importance of considering it as a dynamic and context-bound social practice.

We have made a case for connecting linguistics and organisational studies to make the link between language and organisational realities more visible and actionable. We introduced the central case study, the organisational context, and the participants. We discussed the context of our own work with the team, especially the many identities we assumed or those that were ascribed to us. Working with the team as consultants who needed to provide solutions regarding the communication of the income generation team, as well as academics who were eager to test linguistic-discourse analytic research in organisational contexts, was a balancing act. We hope we managed this act well—the latter effort will surely be judged by the reader of this book.

We are very grateful that we have gained access to and gained the trust of the income generation team. Without them this book could not have been written, and we hope that they will find the analyses and our assessment of their situation insightful. We also consider ourselves lucky that through this consultancy we had the opportunity to conduct scholarly research in a context other researchers may not have access to. This book is, therefore, dedicated to scholars who value emic insights and rich data presented through an interesting story. We hope our experiences and findings can serve as a valuable resource and inspiration for those planning to delve into the intricate world of language and organisational dynamics themselves.

References

Alvesson, M., & Kärreman, D. (2000). Taking the linguistic turn in organizational research: Challenges, responses, consequences. *The Journal of Applied Behavioral Science, 36*(2), 136–158.

Chia, R. (2000). Discourse analysis organizational analysis. *Organization, 7*(3), 513–518.

Cohen, L., Musson, G., & Tietze, S. (2005). Teaching communication to business and management students: A view from the United Kingdom. *Management Communication Quarterly, 19*(2), 279–287.

Darics, E. (2019). Critical language and discourse awareness in management education. *Journal of Management Education, 43*(6), 651–672.

Darics, E. (2020). The relevance of applied linguistic and discourse research: On the margins of communication consultancy. In L. Mullany (Ed.), *Professional communication: Consultancy, advocacy, activism* (pp. 47–64). Springer.

Darics, E., & Clifton, J. (2019). Making applied linguistics applicable to business practice. Discourse analysis as a management tool. *Applied Linguistics, 40*(6), 917–936.

Dyer, W. G., Jr., & Wilkins, A. L. (1991). Better stories, not better constructs, to generate better theory: A rejoinder to Eisenhardt. *Academy of Management Review, 16*(3), 613–619.

Gummesson, E. (2017). *Case theory in business and management: Reinventing case study research.* Sage.

Hacker, P. M. (2013). The linguistic turn in analytic philosophy. In M. Beany (Ed.), *The Oxford handbook of the history of analytic philosophy.* Oxford University Press. https://doi.org/10.1093/oxfordhb/9780199238842.013.0030

Haire, M. (Ed.). (1959). *Modern organization theory.* Wiley.

Jian, G., Schmisseur, A. M., & Fairhurst, G. T. (2008). Organizational discourse and communication: The progeny of Proteus. *Discourse & Communication.*, *2*(3), 299–320.

Kirby, E., & Krone, K. (2002). "The policy exists but you can't really use it": Communication and the structuration of work-family policies. *Journal of Applied Communication Research, 30*(1), 50–77.

Lockwood, C., Giorgi, S., & Glynn, M. A. (2019). "How to do things with words": Mechanisms bridging language and action in management research. *Journal of Management, 45*(1), 7–34.

Lønsmann, D. (2016). Negotiating positionality in ethnographic investigations of workplace settings: Student, consultant or confidante? In G. Alessi & G. Jacobs (Eds.), *The ins and outs of business and professional discourse research: Reflections on interacting with the workplace* (pp. 13–36). Springer.

Marichal, J. (2012). *Facebook democracy: The architecture of disclosure and the threat to public life*. Taylor & Francis

Mautner, G. (2016). *Discourse and management: Critical perspectives through the language lens*. Macmillan.

Mautner, G. (2017). Organizational discourse. In G. Mautner & F. Reiner (Eds.), *Handbook of business communication, linguistic approaches* (pp. 609–628). Mouton De Gruyter.

Murphy, S. A., & O'Brien, A. N. (2006). Listening above the din: The potential of language in organizational research. *International Journal of Qualitative Methods, 5*(2), 87–110.

Musson, G., Cohen, L., & Tietze, S. (2007). Pedagogy and the 'linguistic turn' developing understanding through semiotics. *Management Learning, 38*(1), 45–60.

Pugh, D. S., & Hickson, D. J. (2007). *Writers on organizations* (6th ed.). Sage.

Putnam, L. L., & Fairhurst G. (2001). Discourse analysis in organizations. Issues and concerns. In F. M. Jablin & L. L. Putnam (Eds.), *The new handbook of organizational communication* (pp. 78–136). Sage.

Putnam, L. L., & Mumby, D. K. (2014) Introduction. Advancing theory and research in organizational communication. In L. L. Putnam & D. Mumby (Eds.), *The SAGE handbook of organizational communication* (3rd ed., pp. 1–18). Sage.

Stake, R. E. (1995). *The art of case study research*. Sage.

Stewart, R. (1997). *The reality of management* (3rd ed.). Butterworth-Heinemann.

Musson, G., Cohen, L., & Tietze, S. (2003). *Understanding organizations through language*. Sage.

Vallaster, C. (2000). Conducting field research in Asia: Fundamental differences as compared to Western societies. *Culture & Psychology, 6*(4), 461–476.

CHAPTER 2

Data: Access, Transcription, Analysis

Introduction

This book is based on the idea that organisations are discursive constructions. From this broadly social constructionist perspective, to borrow a metaphor from Potter (1996: 97), language use doesn't merely represent the world as a mirror reflects an image; rather, it is like a construction yard in which the organisation is constituted as people talk it and write it. Consequently, we argue that it is through paying attention to the communicative practices of organisational players that we can make tangible, and therefore analysable, the way in which organisations are communicatively constituted. In this chapter, we set out some key premises behind such an assertion and draw your attention to issues related to data collection, interviewing, transcription, carrying out the analyses, and applying their results to organisational theory and practice.

Gaining Access to a Research Site and Data Collection

Of course, scholars with an interest in exploring organisation and organising through a language lens may use many methods to make the way in which organisations are communicatively constituted tangible—some of which we set out in this book. Central to these methods is the fine-grained

E. Darics and J. Clifton, *Organisation, Communication and Language*, New Perspectives in Organizational Communication,
https://doi.org/10.1007/978-3-031-30199-5_2

analysis of organisational talk or text, and for this scholars need to collect actual talk and text: recordings of naturally occurring conversations, meetings, or interviews, email exchanges, social media interactions, and similar. To obtain such data, researchers and consultants need access to decision-makers who can grant entry into organisations, events that take place, and individuals. We agree with Gummesson (2000: 14), who underlines the importance of access and argues that "traditional research methods used in business research do not provide satisfactory access ... A researcher's or consultant's ability to carry out work on a project is intimately tied up with the availability of data and information that can provide a basis for analysis and conclusions". However, it is not easy to gain access to organisations, especially in business contexts where confidentiality can be a serious hindrance (see, e.g., Holmes & Vine, 2021; Ly, 2016). But even after access is granted, in order to meaningfully assess data in the context of its use, researchers need to gain the trust of the participants (Vallaster, 2000) and develop emic insights into the culture they set out to observe (Darics, 2020). This takes a lot of time and effort, and, as Sarangi (2002: 389) notes, should involve "spending time aimed at not only understanding the work setting, and developing working relationships with practitioners, but also demonstrating long-term commitment to the site".

Our consultancy did not have a generous time allowance, as Sarangi recommends. We were allowed into the organisation for two days. The first informal day was devoted to getting to know the team members and the case: we recorded the interviews and spent time in the office trying to establish a trusting atmosphere, especially through informal discussions about the aims of the research. This was particularly important because the next day we were planning to record the interactions of the core team members throughout their working day. Following these discussions, we were given permission to collect data in the planned way.

In order to record their daily interactions, the participants were equipped with microphones and recording equipment that they carried with them throughout the day and were discreetly attached to their clothing. The decision to turn the microphone on and off was in the hands of the participants—the recording was automatically triggered by noise, so it did not record silent periods. The main advantage of such a process of collecting data was that not only did it have the potential to capture more formal interactions during meetings and so on but it also allowed us to record fewer formal interactions such as "corridor" talk.

We ended up with useable recordings from Dot (240 minutes), Rick (80 minutes), and Amy (210 minutes), although some of the recordings overlapped considering the fact that the team had shared work sessions and meetings.

Since the recording equipment was fairly discreet, a further advantage was that this diminished the observer's paradox whereby "the aim of linguistic research in the community must be to find out how people talk when they are not being systematically observed; yet we can only obtain these data by systematic observation" (Labov, 1972: 209). Consequently, researchers such as Labov argued that, paradoxically, it is impossible to record natural speech when being observed/recorded because when participants are knowingly being recorded this talk is not natural. Some researchers claim that once the recordings are underway, participants forget they are being recorded and therefore the actual recording process has a limited effect on the interaction, which remains relatively natural (e.g. Chan, 2008). Other researchers (e.g. Speer, 2002), while arguing that the presence of recording equipment is not a priori consequential to the interaction, nevertheless point out that the recording equipment indexes the absent presence of a researcher who will later analyse the talk of the participants. Consequently, as the observer's paradox suggests, recorded interaction can never be totally natural.

The team members had reservations about the recording devices to begin with—but the fact that they could switch them off themselves, and that the recording was voice activated, sufficiently reassured them to agree to wearing them. Listening back to the recordings suggested to us that, indeed, team members had forgotten about the devices. This was signalled, for example, by moments of exclamation when they suddenly remembered the devices. Similarly, there were instances when team members became aware of the "absent presence" of the researcher, commenting on how we, as consultants, may perceive their interactions. In Extract 2.1, we see an instance of both cases. Here, the team is getting ready for a meeting with management and, interrupting a conversation about the issues they need to discuss, Amy exclaims: "We are miked up".

Extract 2.1

1.	Amy:	we're miked up (.) supposing they say something really
2.		bad and they say I'm taping <u>you</u>
3.	All:	((Laughter))
4.	Amy:	if I take that off it's SO obvious I'm gonna have to say I've got a mike on

5.	Dot:	well YEAH
6.	Amy:	what you lookin' at this beautiful body Rob↑
7.		I'm not flashing FLASH
8.	All	((Laughter))
9.	Rick:	look good from here! ((Laughs))
10.	Dot:	why don't you tuck it
11.	Amy:	oh why don't I (.) take it off (.) and then (.)w-we can listen via yours
12.		because YOU can't SEE yours, yours is like you- you've got a problem
13.		((Laughs))
14.	Dot:	you're sitting right next to-what d'you mean I've got a problem? ((Laughs))
15.	Amy:	you you can't hear or something mine is so obviously like a mike
16.	Dot:	why don't you go in the (.) like put it through and just wear it there or
17.		something
18.	Amy:	put it through↑ she's like put it through (.) I mean there's no one here
19.		(.) like dangling dangling from (.) through my legs ((Laughs))
20.	All:	((laughter))
21.	Rob:	they're going to listen back (.) dangling stick it through

In Extract 2.1, we see evidence of not only the team members' awareness of the microphones and the future processing of the recording (lines 1 and 21) but also their view of the recording device as a tool to potentially capture sensitive information from upper management. Here, the team members jokingly mention the possibility of using the microphones to their advantage in line 2: "Supposing they say something really bad and they say, 'I'm taping you!'", and go on to discuss how best to conceal the microphone before they enter the meeting. The idea of using the microphones to "spy" on management reflects the participants' perception of the devices—and by extension us as consultants—as tools that can impact power dynamics within the organisation. In the previous chapter, we discussed the different identities consultants may assume or which may be assigned to them. Lønsmann (2016) found that one identity that can be attributed to a consultant is: "spy for the management". The interaction above reveals a different conceptualisation of spying—not for but *on* management. This jocular episode is representative of the divide between the team and upper management, and symptomatic of the deep problems that result from the divide—as we will see later in Chapters 4, 5, and 9.

To return to our discussion about data, generally speaking we can never know the extent to which the researcher's paradox affects an interaction with any certainty. The only way around this dilemma would be to covertly record, which would, of course, be unethical. As a way of addressing, rather than eliminating, this dilemma, Potter (2002) proposes the use of the adjective naturalist*ic*. This allows the researcher to make a distinction between data that is "got up" (i.e. interview talk, talk in experimental venues, focus groups, surveys, and so on, which are designed for research purposes and strongly influenced by these purposes) and data that is not "got up" (i.e. talk that is situated as far as possible in the everyday (workplace) practices of the participants). Thus, following Potter (2002), we consider that the interaction we had access to through the participant recordings was as natural as it could be and allowed us to access the everyday workplace activities of the participants in as discreet a way as possible. While acknowledging debates around the "naturalness" of recorded interaction, in line with Potter's (2002) distinction between data that is "got up" and that which is not, throughout this book we use the term "naturally occurring talk" to describe the recorded data we collected that was not "got up".

Further, what is actually captured on the recording is dependent on the technical limitations of the equipment used and where it is placed. However, despite these constraints, as Sacks (1984: 26) famously noted: "the tape-recorded materials constituted a 'good enough' record of what had happened. Other things, to be sure, happened, but at least what was on the tape had happened". Of course, one of the main "things" that the use of audio-taped data fails to capture is non-verbal aspects of interaction such as eye gaze, gesture, body position, and the interface between participants and artefacts such as computers, telephones, office equipment, and so on. However, for the purposes of this book, the limitations of audio recordings compared to video recordings were a downside that we were prepared to accept as a trade-off in return for the ability to allow the participants to carry the recording equipment with them as they went about their everyday workplace activities, rather than having fixed video cameras in position.

In organisational research, interviews are often used as a method of "getting at" the ways in which participants perceive the organisational landscape. This, as we demonstrate in Chapter 3, can bring significant insights. However, we also note that most organisational work that uses interviews treats the interview itself as an asocial encounter for the transmission of knowledge. In other words, most research treats language as a mirror that provides an accurate window on the pre-discursive "real" world of the organisation that is "out there somewhere" and on the interviewee's state of mind, opinions, and beliefs that are "in there somewhere". Interviewees are thus treated as "repositories of facts, reflections, opinions, and other traces of experience" (Holstein & Gubrium, 2004: 144) which can easily be elicited and transformed into "data" providing care is taken to remain neutral so that the interview process is not contaminated. Moreover, once this "data" is obtained, the interviewee's talk is often coded into researcher categories and then quotes from the interview are picked out to illustrate the coded themes.

While such an approach has no doubt contributed significantly to organisational research, it overlooks the interview as an interactional event. As Potter and Wetherell (1988) convincingly demonstrate, from a discursive perspective, beliefs, opinions, values, and knowledge that are expressed in interviews are discursively constructed in order to attend to the exigencies of the interactional situation and, far from being fixed, are variable, fluid, and sometimes even contradictory. Thus, when interviews are used as a research method, it is important not only to consider them as end products but also to take into account the ways in which they are interactionally co-constructed with the interviewer to talk into being particular versions of the organisational landscape. Thus, as we see in Chapter 3, we consider the interview to be an interactional event and analyse the actual language used by the interviewee as he or she constructs a contextually bound version of the organisation (see also Darics & Clifton [2019] for more on this).

Recordings and Transcription

Once the recordings of the events were made, they then needed to be processed. In the case of this work, confidentiality was a priority. We obtained informed consent and permission to work with and publish extracts from the collected data, but to maintain confidentiality we needed to make the data anonymous. To that end, in the published data we use pseudonyms and have deleted all specific references to people and locations that would make the participants or location recognisable.

Then, the recorded data needed to be transcribed. There are, of course, almost as many ways of transcribing as there are researchers. Bucholtz

(2000) places these methods of transcribing on a continuum of styles which range from so-called naturalised transcription, in which the process is obscured through the adoption of writing conventions such as commas, full stops, capitalisations, the erasure of pauses, hesitations, changes in pitch, and so on, to so-called denaturalised transcription, in which the transcriber attempts to remain more or less faithful to the spoken language by including pauses, hesitations, changes in pitch, and so on. Such a continuum suggests that, as Ochs (1979) pointed out over 40 years ago, transcribing is not a neutral, atheoretical, transparent activity that simply "represents" what was said. Rather, any transcription is a transformation from recording to text and is necessarily selective and dependent on the level of detail required by the disciplinary procedures and traditions that you may ascribe to.

We recommend that you look at Antaki's (n.d.) section on transcription in his tutorial on conversation analysis. In this tutorial, Antaki provides an excellent series of exercises demonstrating how to transcribe and a discussion of the different degrees of detail that a transcription may require. At the end of the day, however, the level of transcription required depends on the exigencies of the research tradition that you decide to use and the assumptions of that tradition. For example, if you are interested in collecting a large corpus of the occurrence of a particular lexical item perhaps, in Bucholtz's (2000) terms, a naturalised transcript may be sufficient. On the other hand, if you are interested in overlapping talk, a more detailed, denaturalised transcription detailing exactly where overlap occurs may be required. In the case of the transcripts presented in this book, we work from a simplified version of the Jeffersonian system (Jefferson, 2004). This, we argue, is sufficient to capture the details of talk, yet at the same time it remains relatively accessible to the reader who is not especially well versed in the granularity of transcription that a full Jeffersonian transcript sometimes requires. See Appendix 1 for a full list of transcription symbols used.

Analysing the Data: Validity, Generalisability, and Reliability

Once the transcript is done it should provide a (good enough) record of the actual workplace practices of the organisational players in and through which the organisation is communicatively constructed. The use of transcripts of naturally occurring workplace interaction and/or authentic organisational texts stands in stark contrast to much research into management and organisation in which interviews, questionnaires, and surveys remain the methods of preference (see Greatbatch & Clark, 2017). While such methods have provided many insights into organisation and organising, the downside of using them to access organisational practices is that they are post hoc methods of data collection that rely on *re*construction, *re*collection, and *re*presentation events. In short, they provide access to what organisational players say they do, not what they actually do.

While we are not claiming that interviewees would deliberately lie, such post hoc *re*constructions, *re*collections, and *re*presentations are necessarily shot through with the management of the positive self-image of the interviewee/respondent. They are also necessarily positioned in relation to what is sayable within the context of the research interview/survey, which is placed in relation to widely circulating discourses of "good" organisational practice. Conversely, research that is based on the analysis of authentic texts and naturally occurring talk allows you to get closer to actual organisational practices. This favours an appreciation of the complexity of human interaction as it actually happens as real time, in situ social practice. The main advantage of using naturally occurring workplace interactions for analysing workplace practices and theoretical constructs of interest to organisational scholars is therefore that they render the act of organising visible and thus analysable.

Scholars who consider quantitative research as the epitome of thorough science may view such fine-grained, often single-case linguistic analyses as lacking in statistical confirmation and therefore running the risk of being statistically insignificant or generalisable. However, we argue that it is precisely in these relatively fine-grained details of interaction that phenomena of interest to organisational scholars (such as power, gender, leadership, etc.) are not only to be found but theorising about these phenomena should be answerable to the details of its actual naturally occurring occurrences. As Schegloff (1987: 102) puts it, "whatever concerns for macro social issues we entertain, our ways of dealing with them will in the end have to be compatible with a capacity to address the details of single episodes of action through talking in interaction". Fine-grained analyses of organisational interaction often—though certainly not always—rely on single-case studies. However, despite such a reliance on single instances, findings can still be considered generalisable. We have two arguments to support this.

First, this is because organisational players organise their talk in orderly ways which have generic qualities. In short, to borrow a metaphor from Sacks (1984), the machinery of talk that is used in one particular event is useable in other similar situations. Further, the reliability and validity of fine-grained linguistic analyses of text or talk are similarly not to be found in the statistical analysis of data. Rather, any claims that an analyst makes should have their warrant in a fine-grained analysis of the transcripts, and the reliability and validity of these claims can be put to the test by fellow academics carrying out their own analyses. Moreover, if need be, access to the transcript makes the analysis replicable.

Second, case study-based qualitative research is "geared to" understanding whether certain patterns are found to exist instead of exploring how often and to what extent. This is what Gummerson calls *analytic generalisation* (Gummesson, 2017: 159). Elsewhere, Gummesson (2000: 89) points out that if analysts are able to describe the "interaction between various parts of the system and the important characteristics of the system, the possibilities to generalize also from very few cases, or even one single case, may be reasonably good". What this means is that in single-case research, we are not seeking generalisability in statistical sampling or cause-and-effect relationships but rather in the thoroughness of the measures and analyses that allow us to reach a "fundamental understanding of the structure, the processes and the driving forces". Such thoroughness is precisely what comprehensive, fine-grained linguistic analyses can offer.

Applying Linguistics to Organisational Practice

As we have argued above, not only do the fine-grained linguistic analyses of text and transcripts of naturally occurring talk provide you with a rigorous way of investigating organisational phenomena, we also argue that the results of such research are relevant for practice. The problem of relevance has been a constant bugbear in much management/organisational research. For example, Dennis Tourish (2019, 2020) has recently relaunched a critique of management research, claiming that much of it is pretentious nonsense because it is too preoccupied with creating the illusion of theory development (Tourish, 2019: 6), and, more specifically in the domain of leadership, Pfeffer (2015) argues that theories such as authentic leadership and servant leadership tell us little about how leadership is enacted in practice. Consequently, it could be argued that management/organisational research fails to provide students and practitioners with the ability to relate research to the day-to-day realities of management practice.

A linguistic approach to organisation and organising offers a way out of this dilemma. This is because analyses of naturally occurring talk and text, and therefore also the outcomes of these analyses, are necessarily based on what actually happens in organisations. Consequently, taking a linguistic approach to the investigation of organisational phenomena has the potential to cut through second-order theoretical constructs of "big" issues, such as leadership, teamwork, decision-making, and so on, and allows us to consider how such issues are actually enacted in talk. The main advantage then of seeking such "big" organisational phenomena in the terra firma of naturally occurring talk and text is that "grand theories" are eschewed in favour of revealing how organisational phenomena are actually accomplished as part of everyday workplace activities. For example, in relation to leadership, Clifton (2006) argues that using the analysis of transcripts of naturally occurring talk helps avoid the pitfalls of providing research that is anchored in grand theories of leadership but which does not necessarily provide findings that help practitioners to "do" leadership. He argues that a language-based approach to leadership, grounded in the analysis of naturally occurring talk, could offer practitioners a tool kit of linguistic resources for doing leadership, bridging any potential gap between the rigour of research and its relevance to practitioners.

Further, in contrast to much communication advice that is already "out there", the findings from language-based research are located in actual practice and therefore have the potential to offer evidence-based advice that is relevant to practitioners. Cameron (2000), for example, famously points out that much advice concerning (organisational) communication is not based on actual observation and description of naturally occurring talk or workplace practice; rather, it is based on classical rhetoric or what she (2000: 32) describes as the "self-improvement tradition". The self-improvement tradition includes both manuals on etiquette, as typified by Dale Carnegie's (1936) book *How to Win Friends and Influence People*, said to be one of the best-selling books of all time, and communication training that is grounded in fashionable concepts, such as emotional intelligence, neuro-linguistic programming, transactional analysis, and so on.

As Cameron (2000) also contends, not only is such advice removed from close observation of actual practice but it is also essentially prescriptive, decontextualised, reductive, and misguided. For example, as Van De Mieroop et al. (2019) demonstrate, the advice you can find in "how-to" books concerning job interviews often directs the reader never to criticise a former employer in a job interview. This, at first glance, may appear sound advice, yet in their analyses of actual interview talk Van De Mieroop et al. (2019), counter-intuitively, demonstrate that criticising a former employee can be a successful strategy. In the real-world data they analyse, they demonstrate how a successful candidate criticised his former employer and, in this case at least, such self-revelation built trust between the interviewee and interviewer. This is not to say that criticising a former employer is a strategy to employ willy-nilly during a job interview, but it is to say that analysing actual communicative practice may encourage language awareness and, through this, promote what could be seen perhaps as the most important ability of a truly skilled communicator which, following Cameron (2000: 179), is "the ability to assess what is going on in a situation and choose [communicative] strategies that are likely to be effective in that situation".

Such an awareness of language use could be obtained in many ways. First, it could be through using teaching materials based on instances of actual talk. Darics and Koller's (2018) textbook *Language in Business, Language at Work* designed for pre-service students provides an excellent example of this. The gross aim of the book is to develop students' awareness of how language works so that they can develop their own communication strategies in an effective and context-sensitive manner. To this end, the book revolves around the analysis of real-world language use in the form of transcripts of naturally occurring workplace interaction and actual business correspondence and corporate communications. This authentic data are then juxtaposed with linguistic theories and methods, such as politeness theory, conversation analysis, and rhetoric, which are used to analyse the talk and text and to build an awareness of language use that students can apply to their own workplace practice.

Second, insights of linguistic research into workplace communication can be made into material that gives advice to the practitioner in an accessible manner. You can find an excellent example of such materials on the website of the Language in the Workplace Project (available at http://www.vuw.ac.nz/lals/lwp.). This advice is the fruit of a well-known project that was carried out by researchers at the School of Linguistics and

Applied Language Studies at Victoria University, New Zealand in collaboration with Immigration New Zealand. The objective of this project was to help improve communications between New Zealand employers and managers and new migrant employees from other cultures. The research was based on an extensive collection of recordings of naturally occurring work-based interactions which was then distilled into a series of online resources for both employees and employers.

Third, language awareness can be developed by practitioners and researchers working together on research projects. This is again demonstrated in the work of the Language and the Workplace Project. Jones and Stubbe (2004), for example, report on the way in which the project, drawing on the notion of reflective practice (Schön, 1983), used recordings of the participants' own talk in order to observe how they communicated, reflect on their own practice, and rethink their professional values and ways of communicating. A further example of how observation of naturally occurring workplace interaction is used as the basis for reflection and training is Stokoe's (2014) pioneering application of conversation analysis to communication training. The Conversation Analytic Role-play Method (CARM) combines the insights of conversation analysis with the use of animated audio and video recordings of real time, actual encounters. The method is thus designed as a means of observing, explaining, evaluating, and ultimately improving communicative practices and policies within organisations.

Applying Linguistics to Organisational Theory

Not only does a linguistic approach to the analysis of naturally occurring text and talk have the potential to feed back into training, it also has the potential to address issues of wider interest to organisational scholars—so-called big themes such as power, gender, leadership, and so on. Different research methods based on the analysis of transcripts of naturally occurring text and talk have different methodological exigencies and so are more, or less, suited to addressing these wider themes you may be interested in. Critical discourse analysis, for example, makes explicit the way in which social context shapes, and is shaped by, wider societal discourses and so often deals with "bigger" themes such as power, race, gender, and so on. Conversation analysis, on the other hand, is often criticised for focusing on the minutiae of talk and its inability to effectively deal with the "bigger" issues (see, e.g., McPhee et al., 2006). Nevertheless, regardless of which particular linguistic approach you may decide to take for analysis, from a broadly speaking social constructionist perspective, since organisations are considered to be discursive constructs, it follows that, as Boden (1994: 4) notes, "when people talk they are simultaneously and reflexively talking their relationships, organisations, and whole institutions into action, or into being". These relationships, organisations, and institutions are necessarily shot through with notions of culture, identity, leadership, group dynamics, power, knowledge formation, and so on—the bread and butter of organisational research. And if these "big" concepts/phenomena have an "existence" or bearing on organisations and organising, they should be observable, and analysable, in the everyday workplace practice of organisational players—if not, they may be revealed to be researchers' second-order constructs that have little relevance to the lived concerns of organisations and those who inhabit them. Thus, each analytical chapter in this book takes in a particular method of analysis of naturally occurring text or talk, and we link the talk and text to wider social theorising on, for example, such "big" issues as change (Chapter 3), leadership (Chapter 4), sense-making (Chapter 5), organisational identity (Chapter 6), team dynamics (Chapter 7), and authority (Chapter 8).

For readers of this book who consider themselves to be more from the field of management and organisational studies, we hope that some of the research methods showcased here may inspire you to work within a linguistic frame and so may bring a new and exciting lens to bear on your work. For readers who come from a linguistic background, we hope that this book may inspire you to look beyond the text and talk and to combine your work with broader themes of interest to organisational research. In short, we see the approach put forward in this book as a bridge between two broadly speaking separate disciplines that to date have largely been talking past each other rather than to each other. We hope that working at the intersection of management/organisational studies and linguistics may go some way to providing a synergy between disciplines which has to date been relatively under-exploited.

Outline of the Book

Each chapter starts with a discussion of a particular method, showcases its use, and establishes a link to a phenomenon of interest to organisational scholars. The chapters are organised so that we learn increasingly more about the fundraising team and the issues they face in the hospice.

We get to experience their unfolding story through the data collected during the consultancy: Chapter 3 explores interview data, Chapters 4, 5, and 7 analyse naturally occurring talk recorded during team meetings, Chapter 6 explores corporate communication text from the company's Twitter account, and Chapter 8 explores a one-to-one interaction between a supervisor and a team member. Interspersed in the book, we introduce data from other contexts, such as informal office chatter (e.g. Extract 2.1) or a voicemail message (Chapter 9).

From Chapter 3 onwards we delve into the unfolding consultancy. Chapter 3 focuses on the accounts of two team members: Amy, the newly appointed head of income generation, and Dot, the longest-serving member of the team. In this chapter, we propose a novel use of metaphor analysis, combining approaches to metaphor from organisational and discourse scholarship. The analysis exposes conceptualisations of organisational culture and gives the first insights into the problems that arose from a badly managed change process. Chapter 4 uses membership categorisation analysis to combine the fine-grained analysis of meeting talk with research on leader identity construction. Thus, as is often the case in leadership research, rather than investigating informants' understanding of leadership and leader identity in research environments that are removed from actual practice, the chapter shows how participants enacted a contextualised and moral understanding of leadership as part of in situ workplace practice which was deployed to "do" things—in this case criticise the top management team. Chapter 5 continues to lay bare the deep frictions in the hospice. Noting that storytelling is a site par excellence for organisational sense-making, the chapter takes a narrative as social practice approach to investigate the telling of rumour during a meeting. In these analyses, we demonstrate how failure to make sense of rumour leads to organisational paralysis.

In Chapter 6, we combine findings of research into organisational identity with metadiscourse analysis to understand the challenges of fragmented organisational identity and its implications on internal coherence and external stakeholder perceptions. The examination of the fundraising team's social media messages reveals that the team's projected identity is ambiguous and fragmented. This realisation is unexpected in the light of the issues uncovered in the previous chapters but showcases how metadiscourse analysis can contribute to a more comprehensive understanding of organisational identity management, particularly during organisational change. Chapter 7 takes a conversation analytic approach to address the rather nebulous concept of team spirit and argues that this method may be able to help us define the "just whatness" of team spirit and contribute to our understanding of how it is achieved as an interactional phenomenon. Focusing on a longer stretch of a decision-making episode between team members, the chapter demonstrates how team spirit is not something the group "has" but rather it is something they "do" through shared laughter, teasing, and self-deprecation. Chapter 8 draws on the Montreal School's notion of ventriloquism and the communicative constitution of the organisation. It considers how authority is enacted in organisations through the ability of certain participants to ventriloquise (i.e. speak on behalf of) non-human entities such as organisational protocols and insurance policies which are attributed agency. Therefore, in this chapter, instead of taking an anthropocentric view of the organisation in which humans determine and control the material world, a ventriloquial approach allows us to consider how the material world of the organisation is talked into being and attributed agency.

References

Antaki, C. (n.d.). *Tutorial on conversation analysis*. Available online at https://learn.lboro.ac.uk/ludata/cx/ca-tutorials/transintro1.htm

Boden, D. (1994). *The business of talk. Organizations in action*. Polity.

Bucholtz, M. (2000). The politics of transcription. *Journal of Pragmatics, 32*(10), 1439–1465.

Cameron, D. (2000). *Good to talk? Living and working in a communication culture*. Sage.

Carnegie, D. (1936). *How to win friends and influence people*. Simon & Schuster.

Chan, A. (2008). Meeting opening and closings in a Hong Kong company. In H. Sun & D. Kádár (Eds.), *It's the dragon's turn: Chinese institutional discourses* (pp. 181–230). Bern Peter Lang.

Clifton, J. (2006). A conversation analytical approach to business communication: The case of leadership. *The Journal of Business Communication, 43*(3), 202–219.

Darics, E. (2020). E-leadership or "how to be boss in instant messaging?" The role of nonverbal communication. *International Journal of Business Communication, 57*(1), 3–29.

Darics, E., & Koller, V. (2018). *Language in business, language at work*. Palgrave.

Darics, E., & Clifton, J. (2019). Making applied linguistics applicable to business practice. Discourse analysis as a management tool. *Applied Linguistics, 40*(6), 917–936.

Greatbatch, D., & Clark, T. (2017). *Using conversation analysis for business and management students*. Sage.
Gummesson, E. (2017). *Case theory in business and management. reinventing case study research*. Sage.
Gummesson, E. (2000). *Qualitative methods in management research* (2nd ed.). Sage.
Holmes, J., & Vine, B. (2021). Workplace research and applications in real world contexts: The case of the Wellington Language in the Workplace Project. In G. Jacobs & S. DeCock (Eds.), *Good data in business and professional discourse research and teaching: Further explorations* (pp. 25–54). Springer.
Holstein, J. A., & Gubrium, J. F. (2004). The active interview. In D. Silverman (Ed.), *Qualitative research: Theory, method and practice* (2nd ed., pp. 140–161). Sage.
Jefferson, G. (2004). Glossary of transcript symbols with an introduction. In G. H. Lerner (Ed.), *Conversation analysis: Studies from the first generation* (pp. 13–31). John Benjamins.
Jones, D., & Stubbe, M. (2004). Communication and the reflective practitioner: A shared perspective from sociolinguistics and organisational communication. *International Journal of Applied Linguistics, 14*(2), 185–211.
Labov, W. (1972). The study of language in its social context. In J. Pride & J. Holmes (Eds.), *Sociolinguistics* (pp. 180–202). Penguin Books.
Lønsmann, D. (2016). Negotiating positionality in ethnographic investigations of workplace settings: Student, consultant or confidante? In G. Alessi & G. Jacobs (Eds.), *The ins and outs of business and professional discourse research: Reflections on interacting with the workplace* (pp. 13–36). Springer.
Ly, A. (2016). Getting access to language data in the workplace: Role enactment as a data-generation method. In G. Alessi & G. Jacobs (Eds.), *The ins and outs of business and professional discourse research: Reflections on interacting with the workplace* (pp. 63–80). Springer.
McPhee, R., Myers, K., & Trethewey, A. (2006). On collective mind and conversational analysis: Response to Cooren. *Management Communication Quarterly, 19*(3), 311–326.
Ochs, E. (1979). Transcription as theory. *Developmental pragmatics, 10*(1), 43–72.
Pfeffer, J. (2015). *Leadership BS: Fixing workplaces and careers one truth at a time*. HarperCollins.
Potter, J. (1996). *Representing reality: Discourse, rhetoric and social construction*. Sage.
Potter, J. (2002). Two kinds of natural. *Discourse Studies, 4*(4), 539–542.
Potter, J., & Wetherell, M. (1988). Accomplishing attitudes: Fact and evaluation in racist discourse. *Text-Interdisciplinary Journal for the Study of Discourse, 8*, 51–68.

Sarangi, S. (2002). Discourse practitioners as a community of interprofessional practice: Some insights from health communication research. In C. Candlin (Ed.), *Research and practice in professional discourse* (pp. 95–136). City University of Hong Kong Press.

Sacks, H. (1984). Notes on methodology. In J. M. Atkinson & J. Heritage (Eds.), *Structures of social action: Studies in conversation analysis* (pp. 2–27). Cambridge University Press.

Schegloff, E. (1987). Analyzing single episodes of interaction: An exercise in conversation analysis. *Social Psychology Quarterly, 50*(2), 101–114.

Schön, D. (1983). *The reflective practitioner*. Basic Books.

Speer, S. (2002). 'Natural' and 'contrived' data: A sustainable distinction? *Discourse Studies, 4*(4), 511–525.

Stokoe, E. (2014). The Conversation Analytic Role-play Method (CARM): A method for training communication skills as an alternative to simulated role-play. *Research on Language and Social Interaction, 47*(3), 255–265.

Tourish, D. (2019). *Management studies in crisis: Fraud, deception and meaningless research*. Cambridge University Press.

Tourish, D. (2020). The triumph of nonsense in management studies. *Academy of Management Learning & Education, 19*(1), 99–109.

Vallaster, C. (2000). Conducting field research in Asia: Fundamental differences as compared to Western societies. *Culture & Psychology, 6*(4), 461–476.

Van De Mieroop, D., Clifton, J., & Schreurs, C. (2019). The interactional negotiation of the rules of the employment interview game: Negative remarks about third parties and "doing" trust. *International Journal of Business Communication, 56*(4), 560–585.

CHAPTER 3

Mother, Machine, Ninja: Analysing Metaphors in Organisational Communication

Introduction

We started the previous chapter with two metaphors borrowed from Potter's (1996) book on representing reality: one compared language to a mirror that "reflects" reality and the other to the construction yard where language constitutes reality. As a starting point for this chapter on metaphors, it will be useful to add the *extended*[1] metaphors Potter (1996: 97–98) uses. Construction, as he argues, can happen at two levels. First, we construct a version of reality as we talk (or write) about it. Second, we also construct our text or talk from elements of language—and as such, these elements can be interchanged or combined differently. This, as Potter (1996: 98) puts it, "emphasises that descriptions are human practices and that descriptions could have been otherwise".

It is very helpful to bear in mind these two types of "constructions" when we start thinking about metaphors. The first meaning is useful to recognise metaphors as conceptual constructions that help us make sense of our (abstract) realities. In this sense, "the locus of metaphor is not language at all, but in the way we conceptualise one mental

[1] This is already a useful concept in understanding metaphorical language: in extended or sustained metaphors the comparison between two seemingly dissimilar things is not only made once but is continued and developed throughout the text.

E. Darics and J. Clifton, *Organisation, Communication and Language*, New Perspectives in Organizational Communication,
https://doi.org/10.1007/978-3-031-30199-5_3

domain in terms of another" (Lakoff & Johnson, 2003: 203). The second meaning—construction as the combining of elements of language—draws attention to how conceptualisations manifest in language. Extract 3.1 from Kira's interview is an example. In this part of the interview, she is retelling her story at the hospice:

Extract 3.1

1.	Kira	so I think that's why I've ended up slotting into that kind of role because um I
2.		feel comfortable going and meeting new people in businesses and talking to
3.		them about, you know, getting involved in stuff so ((audio jumps))
4.		an interesting eight or nine months ((laughs))

If you consider the language in the extract above, it is possible to describe how someone makes sense of and makes the best of a new professional role in a variety of ways. We can, for example, *get a grip on*, *get on with*, *rock*, or, as Kira did, *slot into* a new role. Kira's choice of words evokes an image that professional roles are slots into which, like objects, people can be inserted. The conceptualisation of PROFESSIONAL ROLES AS SLOTS reveals a deeper perspective about how Kira imagines her professional context: slots, like parts working together within a structure (or a machine?) to complete tasks.

A metaphor, as the definition goes, is a "phenomenon whereby we talk and, potentially, think about something in terms of something else" (Semino, 2008: 11). In Extract 3.1, we see that metaphorical language offers a kind of window into Kira's experiences: we may consider that her words reveal how she imagines her organisational reality (her workplace) in terms of a structure or machine. In this chapter, we will explore how language and abstract conceptual realities are interlinked. Specifically, it will examine how language can be used to construct and represent abstract concepts, such as our understanding of professional roles, through the use of metaphors, and demonstrate ways of identifying, analysing, and making sense of metaphors in their broader socio-cultural (specifically here, organisational) context. To do this, first we will provide a brief overview of research on metaphors in organisational scholarship. We will then discuss different approaches to metaphor analysis to demonstrate the utility and importance of paying close attention to naturally occurring text and talk both for researchers and those who can benefit from a better understanding of metaphors in actual work settings. We will show this through the analysis of interview extracts.

We are surrounded by metaphorical language: it structures our perception, forms our conceptual systems, and therefore defines how we view our everyday realities (Lakoff & Johnson, 2003). It is not surprising, therefore, that scholars interested in organisations have taken a keen interest in metaphors, both as a way of theorising (e.g. Alvesson, 2002; Morgan, 1997) and as an analytical tool to study organisations and its stakeholders (see, e.g., Cornelissen et al., 2008; Örtenblad et al., 2016). Theory-focused academic scholarship has influenced an interest in the practical applications and instrumentality of metaphors in achieving organisational aims (Hogler et al., 2008). For example, researchers have considered how to best utilise metaphors in change management (e.g. Akin & Palmer, 2000; Dunford & Palmer, 1996); leadership (Aupperle & Karimalis, 2001; Vignone, 2012); diversity management (Kirby & Harter, 2003); or negotiations (Smith, 2005).

It is not our aim to provide a comprehensive overview of the research on metaphors in organisational scholarship: for such an overview, we recommend Cornelissen and colleagues' (2008) review article, as well as Örtenblad, Trehan, and Putnam's edited collection (2016). Despite the evidently burgeoning field, we have two good reasons to start this case book with metaphor analysis. The first is an academic one: the goal we have set out in the book is to demonstrate what language-focused, close analytical approaches can offer to organisational research—in this instance, to demonstrate how applied metaphor research can further existing approaches to metaphors in organisational scholarship and management practice. We are, of course, not alone in this endeavour; rather, we recognise we are joining previous calls for organisational scholarship to make greater efforts to incorporate the implications of metaphor analysis into language-focused disciplinary areas (Hogler et al., 2008; Inns, 2002; Latusek & Vlaar, 2015; Oswick et al., 2004; Wittink, 2011). The other reason for beginning this book with metaphor analysis is a more practical one, namely that it was in the metaphorical language that we spotted and identified the first symptom of the deep problems in the fundraising team.

Studying Metaphors in Organisational and Discourse Research

Even a cursory overview of metaphor research in organisational contexts will lead you back to Gareth Morgan's (1997) seminal work titled *Images of Organization*, in which he explores the different metaphors and images people use to conceptualise organisations. The book presents a series of metaphors—machines, organisms, brains, cultural systems, political systems, psychic prisons, instruments of domination, and flux and transformation. Morgan (1997) argues that these metaphors provide a unique way of understanding and describing organisations, and that they can be used to highlight different aspects of organisational behaviour and functioning. His work laid the groundwork for an entire tradition that explores organisational phenomena through metaphorical lenses (see Örtenblad et al., 2016).

As Cornelissen et al. (2008: 9) have highlighted, this tradition represents a "decontextualised" approach to metaphors whereby they are "projected" on to organisational realities. Such "projected focus on metaphor", as the authors explain, is necessary because the "purpose of much theorising is essentially to identify and abstract 'second-order' constructs" that are used, primarily, for theory building. An often critiqued shortcoming of such an approach is the "tendency to lock categories into fixed meaning and relationships" (Putnam et al., 1996: 378), a view that, as we will see below, tends to ignore not only the context in which metaphors occur but also the very people who use them.

A different kind of approach that Cornelissen et al. (2008) identify is a "contextual" one in which scholars examine the use, meaning, and impact of metaphors in the context of people's actual language use. The goal of such research is to understand how metaphors are used symbolically and interpretively in people's communication and sense-making. Perren and Atkin's (1997) study of the discourse of owner-managers is a good example of such an approach. In their research, 17 owner-managers from a variety of businesses in the UK were interviewed. The interviews were transcribed and analysed using intuitive metaphor identification. The identified metaphors were grouped together and categorised until patterns emerged. Here, metaphors were treated as "data" that could provide insight into organisational reality, and although the linguistic expressions examined did originate in empirical, real-life texts, their discursive embeddedness, and contextual nature were not considered.

Talking of discursive embeddedness, the contextual nature and linguistic manifestation of metaphors offer us a way into the study of metaphors from a linguistic discourse viewpoint. Metaphors have been extensively studied across various subfields of linguistics and discourse analysis, resulting in a vast area of scholarship which we can only fleetingly mention here. Such mention will not do this complex field justice. Rather, our main goal is to make a case for, and demonstration of, a contextual, language-in-use analysis of metaphor, and show how such analysis offers scope to understand people's conceptions of abstract organisational realities. In linguistics and discourse research, cognitive approaches, exemplified by Lakoff and Johnson's (2003) conceptual metaphor theory, focus on the cognitive processes that underlie the creation and comprehension of metaphors. Such a focus on metaphors in thought is what we have described above as a decontextualised approach to metaphors, as typified in Morgan's (1997) work. Much discourse analytic research, however, expands this original theory by advocating a language-in-use approach (e.g. Cameron & Low, 1999). The argument, as Gibbs (2017: 263) puts it, is that "conceptual metaphors do not sit individually in some mental cabinet, waiting to be activated and then mechanically applied in a generic way for each and every interpretive act. Instead, conceptual metaphors are always articulated in slightly different ways in each context". Contextual situatedness, both in terms of the speaker's socio-cultural background and the specific context of language-in-use, is crucial here. This is precisely where discourse analytic/linguistic approaches can extend the horizons of metaphor research in organisation studies, by encouraging researchers and practitioners to consider metaphors in their complexity within their evolving discursive context. This is what we will demonstrate below.

Metaphor-Led Discourse Analysis: From Language to Thought and Social Reality

The method of identifying, analysing, and connecting language to thought and social reality has been a site of much heated debate, labelled as "rivalry" (Kövecses, 2019) and even "war" (Gibbs, 2017). The latter work takes stock of the developments of the field and is worth consulting for those interested in the different approaches to metaphor analysis. It is worth mentioning one of the best-known methods, developed by a group of scholars collectively named Pragglejaz, called the Metaphor Identification Procedure or MIP (2007) and an extended version developed by Steen and colleagues titled MIPVU (Steen et al., 2010). These methods allow for the systematic analysis of texts whereby each lexical unit is individually examined and a decision about its metaphorical nature is made. These approaches assume that the conceptual metaphors that are manifested in linguistic form are shared between speakers to allow for analytical work that aims to explore the frequency of metaphors and the distribution of metaphorical meaning across large amounts of different kinds of texts.

The focus of the approach we demonstrate below is different. It proposes the examination of metaphors in their real discursive contexts. The reason for this is that different contextual situations or communities may affect how metaphors are used, negotiated, and processed: even the same linguistic text can have different communicative functions or readings depending on the contextual situation (Navarro i Ferrando, 2019) or on the interactional history and group norms between members of various socio-cultural groups (Cameron & Low, 1999). Even Lakoff and Johnson (2003: 230) advocate a perspective in which "understanding emerges from interaction, from constant negotiation with the environment and other people". Consequently, if organisational research is concerned with what metaphors reveal about a participant's ideas and values, or indeed a group's values and culture as they manifest in everyday talk and text, attention needs to be paid to both the close linguistic context within which the linguistic metaphor occurs as well as the discursive practice and its broader socio-cultural context. This requires a change in the researcher's perception, moving from viewing metaphors as static constructs shared by the speakers to a fluid view of metaphors (both conceptual and linguistic), which emerge in a specific context and are open to change.

To illustrate this, let's revisit our discussion about Extract 3.1 where we commented on Kira's conceptualisation of PROFESSIONAL ROLES AS SLOTS, which are part of the bigger structure of the organisation. Earlier we considered her language use as some sort of "window" into her thinking. However, consider that a couple of minutes earlier in the interview she says:

Extract 3.2

1. Kira um, and then my experience here has been quite interesting because I came
2. in as a consultant for three months then they renewed it and because of
3. the changes that they had here in the structure, at one point I was almost
4. presumed to be in charge of a room that I wasn't officially given the job for

This extract reveals that a *structure* conceptualisation has already surfaced in the interaction, especially in the context of the change process. Zooming even further out and drawing on data from the other interviews (see below) and everyday interactions (see data from Chapter 5), we notice that the organisational change was part of a corporate restructuring exercise, throughout which the term *structure* was repeatedly used. This example shows how ideas through metaphors can be imposed on a discourse community (in fact, such instrumentalism inherent in metaphors has already been critically commented on in organisational scholarship, e.g. Hogler et al., 2008) and that ideas and metaphors pass from one speaker to another (Cameron et al., 2009). Driven by this realisation, researchers should become mindful of, for example, how metaphors can be, or could have been, introduced in an interactional situation, and how their meaning is negotiated, accepted, or contested. For example, researchers can see how the use of metaphors in an interview question can impose metaphorical thinking on the participants, or how broader circulating discourses in an organisation can affect the language use of organisational members. The importance of the closer and broader discourse context and the in situ negotiation of meaning in interactions is repeatedly emphasised in this book. For example, in Chapter 4, we show how pronoun use (us and them) talks a divided organisation into being, and in Chapter 7, we see how improprieties and joint laughter can enact team spirit.

Now that we have established the importance of considering the linguistic and discursive context of the observed metaphors, we can move on to the method of analysing and making sense of metaphors in the broadest socio-cultural/organisational contexts. Metaphor-led discourse analysis, as Cameron et al. (2009: 70) propose, is "an interactive and recursive process that keeps moving between evidence in the transcribed talk and the bigger picture". Such analysis, as they argue, is neither inductively bottom-up, thus focusing exclusively on linguistic manifestations of metaphors, nor is it deductively top-down, i.e. assuming that every instance of metaphor in speech reflects underlying conceptual metaphors.

Interactivity and recursivity form a basis of such a "dual" approach (proposed also by Wittink, 2011), in which phases of elicitation and deduction follow each other iteratively. In the elicitation phase, researchers take a bottom-up approach where they analyse language used by organisational members to identify metaphors that are being used naturally in communication. These metaphors can then be used to gain insights into how individuals understand and make sense of their experiences within the organisation. In the projecting phase, researchers draw on conceptual metaphors previously discussed in organisation theory to interpret organisational phenomena. This is a top-down approach whereby researchers apply their theoretical understanding of metaphors to make sense of the data.

In this chapter, we analyse the metaphors as they occurred in the interview data of the two key members of the fundraising team: Amy, the new manager, and Dot, the previous interim manager. Through the analysis of this data, we aim both to demonstrate the importance of the contextual situatedness of metaphors and to exemplify the application of a metaphor-driven discourse analysis based on the dual approach of elicitation and projection.

The concrete steps of our analysis were as follows. First, after the transcription of the data, we manually processed it. In the two interviews analysed in the section, our intuition was strongly influenced by scholarship on conceptual metaphors in organisations, specifically literature that explores the abstract conceptualisation of a company (Morgan, 1997; Smith & Eisenberg, 1987). This was an initial projection phase. Next, we looked for and identified connected linguistic metaphors that co-occurred with the main concepts. These included explicit mappings (e.g. *we were a real family kind of team*) and other metaphorical language (e.g. *we were close-knit*). While engaging with the textual data at a micro-level, we searched for other linguistic metaphors as well as less obvious "process" metaphors, which were stretches of language that could be processed metaphorically by the participants (Cameron & Low, 1999). This was our elicitation phase. Once we had explored the linguistic micro-level, we juxtaposed our observations with the context of the discourse event—we have shown an example of this in Extract 3.2. Finally, zooming out again, we considered what the manifestations of metaphorical thinking can reveal about the ideas and values of the individuals and how these interpretations may affect the team. Considering that this project was part of a consultancy aiming to improve the efficiency of the fundraising team, the latter goal had a critical implication on the outcome of our work.

Data Analysis

Our first noticing of the metaphors happened prior to the actual transcription of the data. Since the brief for our initial consultancy was very vague, we started off our work with the team by interviewing them about their role and what they wanted to get out of the consultancy. The interviews were one to one and semi-structured, which allowed us enough flexibility to probe any topic that we deemed useful for our work at hand. It was during these 20–30-minute interviews that we noticed an emerging pattern in linguistic metaphors. This, of course, was a very intuitive stage but nonetheless influenced, for example, how we formulated our interview questions to avoid confirming or resisting the metaphors our participants used.

In the excerpt below, Amy, the newly appointed director of fundraising, discusses the target income she and her team needs to generate for the hospice. This is where we join the conversation.

Extract 3.3. Interview with Amy, director of income generation

Amy	what was your question↑ my role okay my role is director of
	fundraising and retail in terms of goal is to bring in the one point six
	million for fundraising and the one point three for retail that's what it is
Int	okay have you got any techniques that you developed to motivate the
	people and make sure that you achieve that goal↑ how do you do it↑
Amy	how do I do it it↑ erm what I try to aim what I personally
	believe is eighty percent is structure the rest is personality an=and
	bringing your own authenticity or whatever is to it but I believe that
	you that the organisation must be structured ermm so what that means
	is that there needs to be a plan and people needs to understand the plan
	erm they need to understand their roles they need to understand what
	support they can expect and what is part of their own what they have
	been paid to do erm
Int	so you think your main role is to develop that understanding
Amy	my main role is to develop an understanding, to create the structure
	erm erm so for me for me an organisation, the most important
	thing is that if somebody leaves everything still carries on because of
	the structure and the way forward is owned by the hospice NOT by the
	individual individual brings their own creativity to that role or
	particular strength or weakness but they don't own that that particular

(continued)

(continued)

situations my experience is that it takes about three years to really change that how I do that I literally meet everybody and I if I if I call if I call myself something I call myself the manipulator ninja 'course I AM an manipulator with good intention but I will get I will try and persuade you why we have to do that but I will still use the hierarchy to also make that happen erm we say in fundraising we're not there yet in retail we're definitely not there yet erm euh combination of saying this has to has to happen and meeting everyone to explain or to hear why they think it can't happen so so my view is if I can change the person to even accept change will happen very quickly but to do that takes you have to have that personal interaction and the structure for me creates fairness as well

In Amy's interview extract linguistic metaphors can be clustered around three conceptualisations:

Organisation is structure. This metaphor is very prevalent due to explicit mapping such as *80% is structure*, *organisation must be structured*, and *create a structure*. In the linguistic metaphor *everything carries on*, the physical movement of carrying or moving something forward is mapped on to the abstract concept of resilience (see Kriegsmann-Rabe et al., 2022). Here, *structure* is provided as the reason for *everything carrying on*, so conceptually the organisation as structure provides a foundation that can withstand challenges. The structure as an active agent is also represented in line 32 where it *creates* something—fairness. Taken together, the explicitness and prevalence of this metaphor, drawing on organisation theory (e.g. Morgan, 1997), make this a noteworthy conceptual metaphor to consider. We will do that in the next section.

Competencies/roles are possessions. The phrases *bring your authenticity* and *bring your creativity* suggest that these qualities are possessions that can be carried and brought to a situation. Similarly, the idea of employees *owning their part* or *not owning a particular situation*, and the company owning the way *forward*, uses the language of ownership. The verb *use* in the utterance "use the hierarchy" also implies a possession—in this case the hierarchy—that can be utilised for specific purposes.

Change agent as ninja. *I am a manipulative ninja* is an unconventional metaphor (Kövecses, 2010). The distinction between conventional and unconventional metaphors is that conventional metaphors are characterised by their familiarity and unobtrusiveness while unconventional metaphors are distinguished by their originality and ability to draw attention to themselves. Kövecses (2010) notes that conventionality is not a dichotomy but rather a continuum, and he distinguishes between unconventional linguistic and conceptual metaphors. Evoking the concept of a covert agent who is skilled in martial arts and known for their stealth and agility, Amy uses the *ninja* metaphor to describe her role as a change agent within the organisation. The adjective *manipulator* specifies the context in which the persuasion and influence play an important role in addition to the metaphorical agility and stealth of a ninja. Because this is an unconventional metaphor with potential to interpret *ninja* as a metaphor with different kinds of mappings (e.g. paid mercenary, ruthless) or with a potentially problematic connotative meaning (e.g. stealthy, combative), Amy goes on to expand it by clarifying that she is a *manipulator with good intentions*. We will comment later on Amy's metaphorical language representing her role in the change.

We now move on to Dot's account. Dot is currently a direct report of Amy's, but, unlike Amy, she has lived through the changes that took place at the hospice.

Extract 3.4

1.	Dot:	so I joined a team of. (.) then we became six so another guy joined
2.		with me um and we were a real family kind of team the um head of
3.		fundraising was a bit like kind of mum of everyone type of thing we
4.		were kind of on a-a limb, we were away from everyone so we were
5.		very very close-knit and we worked very well together. I don't (.) I
6.		wouldn't say we were particularly efficient we were probably efficient
7.		putting on events but we weren't efficient as a as a money-making
8.		kind of machine as it were so, although we were (.)we did communicate
9.		pretty well but it was very informal it was very (.) it wasn't very
10.		business-like but it was a nice environment but because we were out
11.		and away from everywhere else we were very much cut off from everybody
12.		so we didn't really we didn't go onto the ward we didn't really see many
13.		people although to get to the main hospice we used to walk through
14.		the old Day Care so with patients we had the rapport which is really

(continued)

(continued)

15.		nice and we've had to really work hard to recreate that over in
16.		the (.) have you been to the centre (.) someone give you a tour round↑
17.	Interv:	no
18.	Dot:	okay right we'll (.) that's really important
19.	Interv:	okay
20.	Dot:	actually really important because it's really really changed even
21.		in just five years we've gone from this, um, kind of cottage
22.		hospital type of feel which was just about still there when I was here and it's
23.		kind of grown they've (.) and the whole demolishing it was like
24.		fundraising was demolished bit by bit the building we were moved
25.		into a very very small room not the room we're in now the whole
26.		building all our quirky building where we were very comfortable had
27.		all our posters up and everything was just completely flattened and
28.		that was like the beginning of the okay, things are going to change

In Dot's account, we can group linguistic metaphors according to three broad conceptualisations:

> **Team is family.** The prominence of the family metaphor is obvious due to explicit mappings such as *we were a real family kind of team* and metaphorical expressions like *close-knit*. Dot also expanded the metaphor by referencing members of the family in *head of fundraising was a bit like kind of a mum of everyone type of thing*. She contrasts her family metaphor with ORGANISATION AS MACHINE, where the latter is efficient in making money and professional, whereas the former is all about emotional connection and working well together. If we explore the close linguistic context of the metaphors in this cluster, we see that Dot invests some effort into her linguistic choices to lessen the strength of the TEAM AS FAMILY metaphorical language. Apart from *close-knit*, which is strengthened by the repeated use of the adverb *very, very*, other metaphorical mappings are mitigated through a series of devices, such as *bit like*, *kind of*, and *type of thing*. The idiomatic qualifier term *as it were* in line 8 is explicit in signalling that Dot is well aware of the metaphorical language she is using. This phrase shows evidence that she used the metaphor for a specific communicative purpose in the context of the interview, perhaps to make the contrast more dramatic for the hearer or to signal her awareness of the broader expectations for efficiency in the hospice.

Sense of isolation as physical locality. In her description, Dot describes physical separation using the metaphorical expressions *being on the limb* and *being cut off*. These expressions use physical space or locality to describe isolation and vulnerability, and in Dot's account, this is mapped on their perceived organisational reality of being separate and isolated from the other departments of the hospice. Further on, she expands the metaphor when she tells her story of the relocation, as we will see below.

Organisational change is demolition. In this section, Dot explains the move from the old office into a new building, and as her storytelling progresses she increasingly adopts the metaphor of change as destruction or demolition. Here, metaphor is not confined to one word but encompasses the whole section, where the old *kind of cottage hospital type of feel, the quirky old building where we were very comfortable* is *demolished, flattened* and they were *moved into a very, very small room.* This is an example of what Steen (2009) calls a deliberate metaphor because it makes intentional use of something to force the listener to think about something else. Here, Dot explicitly compares the organisational restructuring to demolition, saying *it was like fundraising was demolished bit by bit*, and then she expands the metaphor over a longer stretch of talk.

Discussion: Making Sense of and Linking the Findings Within the Broader Social Context

Metaphors of Organisational Reality

As we explained earlier, it was hard not to notice the metaphors that our interviewees fell back on to conceptualise the organisation, its working, and their roles in it. Amy's metaphor was ORGANISATION IS STRUCTURE; Dot's was ORGANISATION IS FAMILY. In Morgan's work (1997), different images/metaphors are proposed as a way of "framing" organisations, among which MACHINE is one of the most prominent. When conceptualising an organisation as a machine the focus falls on the mechanical way of operating where organisational life is routinised and, as Morgan (1997) notes, employees in essence are expected to behave like parts of the machine. Amy's liking of the company to a STRUCTURE provides an insight into exactly such thinking. The metaphor she uses brings with it assumptions such as precisely defined parts (roles), architecture (plan), strength and stability (helps sustain things), and even a level of interchangeability between the elements (workforce), as she implies in "if somebody leaves everything still carries on because of the structure". The influence of this conceptualisation, and how the team espoused the metaphor, is evident in our pull quote too, in which Amy's direct report—and one of the youngest members of the team—talks about *slotting into* her new role, just like a well-oiled part in the big company machine.

Contrast the STRUCTURE metaphor with those found in Dot's account. She does explicitly use the word "family" as a way of describing the work team before the company reorganisation took place, but she also elaborates this metaphor by talking about her boss as a *mum*, using adjectives like *close-knit* (which is typically used in community- or family-related words). An organisation as family presupposes a more informal and relaxed culture where camaraderie and support have central importance. Even though, as we have shown above, her hedging language signals that she wants to downplay the strength of the metaphor, the contrast with Amy's metaphorical language points to a deep conflict between the thinking of these two employees.

Such contrast in how employees of the same organisation conceptualise their institution has in previous research been found to have detrimental effects. Smith and Eisenberg (1987) explored this problem in the context of Disneyland in 1984 in a conflict that led to a month-long strike by employees. Using interviews and metaphor elicitation techniques, the researchers found that what on the surface looked like disagreement over policies and procedures was in fact a disagreement about underlying conceptualisations. Management's emphasis on "DRAMA" and the "business of show business" shed light on the central concepts of conformity, efficiency, and concerns for the bottom line. This, as Smith and Eisenberg noted (1987: 377), was "incompatible with the employees' emphasis on FAMILY, which suggested a transcendence of structure and uncritical support of fellow employees". In our case, therefore, the conceptualisations raise questions about how such differences affect organisational culture, communication, and, from the consultancy's point of view, effective collaboration.

Metaphors of Change

Amy's unconventional metaphor of comparing herself to a ***manipulative ninja*** is interesting and revealing on a close linguistic level and a conceptual level too. Above, we have noted that following the use of the metaphor Amy expands on it to clarify her good intentions. The paragraph that follows, in fact, contains other clarifications, and although not metaphorical in nature these are worth noting for how she presents decision-making and persuasion. She says that *she will try and persuade* but still *use the hierarchy*; she explains top-down decision-making, saying *this has to happen*, mitigated by efforts of *meeting everyone to explain or to hear why*. Later on, she describes that her role is to *change the person to even accept change will happen very quickly* through personal interactions. It is clear from the above that her discursive struggles represent a conflict between top-down orders, changing employees' minds, and at the same time creating an (image of) a democratic group with personal connections where others' views are listened to. The NINJA metaphor can be viewed as a linguistic manifestation of this struggle: because it is unconventional, it takes greater cognitive effort to process, and due to the multifaceted nature of the concept of ninjas, it is open to many interpretations (some of which Amy evidently foregoes).

Why does the language used by Amy, describing her role as a change agent, matter in the context of organisational scholarship? It matters because the success of organisational change depends heavily on how organisational members understand it. Studies have shown that metaphorical language has a direct impact on this understanding. Previous research has explored the instrumental use of metaphors in change management (Akin & Palmer, 2000; Palmer & Dunford, 1996), metaphors as analytical tools to trace organisational sense-making about change (Argaman, 2008), and the role of metaphors in describing the change agent and change process (Cassell & Lee, 2012; Marshak, 2001), all of which are pertinent to our case study. The latter studies focus on the language that change agents use to describe their roles and conclude that the image of the change agent has a direct effect on how the organisation understands the change. For instance, if change is conceptualised as BUILDING or DEVELOPING, then the change agent is represented as a TRAINER, COACH, or DEVELOPER (Marshak, 2001). Therefore, turning back to Amy's metaphor, the depiction of a NINJA as a change agent raises questions about the type or intended change envisioned, which could be in line with the conceptualisation of change as warfare (cf. Cassell & Lee, 2012). If, indeed, change is perceived as warfare in our case study, what are the consequences for (change) management and leadership?

Metaphors of Organisational Restructuring

In the previous section, we raised the question of how Amy conceptualised the change process. In Dot's account, we get a clear picture of her conceptualisation. As identified in the analysis, she progressively uses physical demolition as a metaphor to talk about organisational restructuring. The importance of the closer (physical) environment and its role in affecting discourse becomes evident here. The fundraising team did physically move, and their old building was in fact demolished. In previous research, physical settings have been found to trigger extensions of existing conventional conceptual metaphors and "cause the speaker or conceptualizer to choose a metaphorical expression that best fits that setting, no matter how unconventional it may seem" (Kövecses, 2010: 296). This means that Dot's choice of forceful and illustrative language may have been inspired by the actual events onsite.

Whether inspired by her close physical surroundings or not, Dot's use of a deliberate metaphor indicates that she was discursively constructing the process to enable the interviewers to understand it in the context of demolition and being forcefully moved away from a comfortable environment into an uncomfortable space. This language leads us to consider how organisational members experienced the change, how it made them feel, and what it meant for the effectiveness of the newly formed team.

Conclusion: Metaphors in Practice

Steen and colleagues' book (2010: 1) starts with the statement that "metaphor is a booming business". Although probably not meant literally in the context of academic research, harnessing the power of metaphors is indeed a widely accepted management practice. Utilising metaphors in leadership has been promoted by management scholars (Akin & Palmer, 2000; Aupperle & Karimalis, 2001), consultants, and practitioners (Chowdhury, 2021; Creed & Nacey, 2021) alike. Although some scholars take issue with such instrumentalism (Hogler et al., 2008), the truth is that metaphors are powerful tools for sense-giving and can indeed make a difference in management and in organisational life. Noticing and acting on them is particularly important when different conceptual metaphorical thinking occurs in an organisation, leading to uncertainty and conflict about further actions (Marshak, 2001; Smith & Eisenberg, 1987).

As discussed earlier, understanding metaphors requires a deep knowledge of the discourse environment and a consideration of both the closer and wider context. Therefore, as Latusek and Vlaar (2015: 227) caution, "the instrumental use of metaphor as unambiguous and definite should not be taken for granted". Greater awareness of the complexity of metaphors and research can aid this process. This chapter advocates an approach to organisational research and practice that considers the growing scholarship on metaphor analysis from a linguistic-discourse analytic perspective. We propose an approach that combines elicitation, which involves analysing real text and talk in a close, contextual manner, with projection, which involves projecting metaphors on to organisational realities and enabling further theorisations (Cornelissen et al., 2008).

However, as we have seen in the discussion above, the interpretation of metaphors relies heavily on closer and wider context and requires deep knowledge of the discourse environment. This is where greater awareness of the complexity of metaphors and research can help. In this chapter, we have argued for organisational research and practice to have greater consideration for the burgeoning scholarship on metaphor analysis from a linguistic-discourse analytic perspective. We proposed an approach that combines elicitation, when we examine real text and talk and conduct a close, contextual analysis of metaphors, with projection, whereby metaphors are "projected" on to organisational realities, imposing classifications and enabling further theorisations (Cornelissen et al., 2008).

To put this into practice, we suggest doing the following:

- Look for linguistic metaphors, explicit mappings, and extended metaphorical expressions in the data based on knowledge of decontextualised metaphors in organisational research.
- Extend the search to other metaphors not explicitly drawn from organisational theory.
- Consider metaphors, whether a single lexical item or a longer stretch of text, in their close linguistic and broad discourse and socio-cultural context of use. As a way of prompting such consideration, researchers should ask questions about whether and how

the metaphor was introduced, for example, as part of conscious leadership communication efforts (e.g. Argaman, 2008; Vignone, 2012), or consider if and why metaphors were used consciously or deliberately in text (Steen, 2010).
- Trace back metaphorical expressions to conceptualisations and how they relate to organisational realities.

By following these phases of projection–elicitation–close analysis–projection, we identified three critical issues in the fundraising team: the tension between two differing conceptualisations of the organisation, the consequences of conceptualising change as warfare, and the importance of metaphorical language not only as a means of gaining insight into people's minds but also their feelings. These issues could become valid research questions, as attested by previous research, but they are also crucially important for consultancy because they:

1. address differences in conceptualisation to ensure effective collaboration;
2. understand how/why warfare is a damaging metaphor to guide sense-making;
3. respond to the deep emotions and organisational hurt that employees' stories revealed.

While systematic metaphor analysis applied to longer stretches of transcribed data or written text may be laborious, such work has tremendous benefits for both management practice and consultancy. By working with data, identifying and examining metaphors, and developing heightened metaphor awareness, professionals can spot metaphors in situ as they are being used. As a result of this sensitivity, professionals are better positioned to react on the spot, highlighting, discussing, and (when needed) challenging concepts and beliefs that might otherwise remain hidden below the radar (Creed & Nacey, 2021: 330). It was precisely this sensitivity that drew our attention to the abundance of metaphors during the consultancy, allowing us to shift our attention away from the original brief of "effective communication in the fundraising team" to much deeper issues related to problematic change management and organisational sense-making. The next chapter will examine rumours from the hospice, which will shed more light on these issues.

References

Akin, G., & Palmer, I. (2000). Putting metaphors to work for change in organizations. *Organizational Dynamics, 28*(3), 67–79.

Argaman, E. (2008). In the same boat? On metaphor variation as mediating the individual voice in organizational change. *Applied Linguistics, 29*(3), 483–502.

Aupperle, K., & Karimalis, G. (2001). Using metaphors to facilitate cooperation and resolve conflict: Examining the case of Disneyland Paris. *Journal of Change Management, 2*(1), 23–32.

Cameron, L., & Low, G. (Eds.). (1999). *Researching and applying metaphor* (Cambridge Applied Linguistics). Cambridge University Press.

Cameron, L., Maslen, R., Todd, Z., Maule, J., Stratton, P., & Stanley, N. (2009). The discourse dynamics approach to metaphor and metaphor-led discourse analysis. *Metaphor and Symbol, 24*(2), 63–89. https://doi.org/10.1017/CBO9781139524704

Cassell, C., & Lee, B. (2012). Driving, steering, leading, and defending: Journey and warfare metaphors of change agency in trade union learning initiatives. *The Journal of Applied Behavioral Science, 48*(2), 248–271.

Chowdhury, R. (2021). An appreciation of metaphors in management consulting from the conceptual lens of holistic flexibility. *Systems Research and Behavioral Science, 38*(1), 137–157.

Cornelissen, J. P., Oswick, C., Thøger Christensen, L., & Phillips, N. (2008). Metaphor in organizational research: Context, modalities and implications for research—Introduction. *Organization Studies, 29*(1), 7–22. https://doi.org/10.1177/0170840607086634

Creed, A., & Nacey, S. (2021). Metaphor analysis in vocational counselling: Moving from intuitive to reliable metaphor identification. *British Journal of Guidance & Counselling, 49*(3), 321–332.

Dunford, R., & Palmer, I. (1996). Metaphors in popular management discourse: The case of corporate restructuring. In D. Grant & C. Oswick (Eds.), *Metaphors and organizations* (pp. 95–109). Sage.

Gibbs, R. W. (2017). *Metaphor wars: Conceptual metaphors in human life.* Cambridge University Press.

Hogler, R., Gross, M. A., Hartman, J. L., & Cunliffe, A. L. (2008). Meaning in organizational communication: Why metaphor is the cake, not the icing. *Management Communication Quarterly, 21*(3), 393–412.

Kirby, E. L., & Harter, L. M. (2003). Speaking the language of the bottom-line: The metaphor of "managing diversity." *The Journal of Business Communication, 40*(1), 28–49.

Kövecses, Z. (2010). *Metaphor: A practical introduction.* Oxford University Press.

Kövecses, Z. (2019). Some consequences of a multi-level view of metaphor. In I. Navarro & I. Ferrando (Eds.), *Current approaches to metaphor analysis in discourse* (pp. 19–33). De Gruyter.
Kriegsmann-Rabe, L. M., Hiebel, N., Maus, K., & Geiser, F. (2022). "Flying over the crisis": A study on interdisciplinary metaphors of resilience. *Culture & Psychology, 29*(1), 157–176. https://doi.org/10.1177/1354067X221111438
Lakoff, G., & Johnson, M. (2003). *Metaphors we live by* (2nd ed.). University of Chicago Press.
Latusek, D., & Vlaar, P. W. (2015). Exploring managerial talk through metaphor: An opportunity to bridge rigour and relevance?. *Management Learning, 46*(2), 211–232.
Inns, D. (2002). Metaphor in the literature of organizational analysis: A preliminary taxonomy and a glimpse at a humanities-based perspective. *Organization, 9*(2), 305–330.
Marshak, R. J. (2001). Managing the metaphors of change. *Reflections, 2*(3), 6–15. https://doi.org/10.1162/152417301570338
Morgan, G. (1997). *Images of organization* (2nd ed.). Sage.
Navarro i Ferrando, I. (Ed.). (2019). *Current approaches to metaphor analysis in discourse* (Ser. Applications of cognitive linguistics volume 39). Walter De Gruyter GmbH. https://doi.org/10.1515/9783110629460
Örtenblad, A., Trehan, K., & Putnam, L. L. (Eds.). (2016). *Exploring Morgan's metaphors: Theory, research, and practice in organizational studies*. Sage.
Oswick, C., Putnam, L. L., & Keenoy, T. (2004). Tropes, discourse and organizing. In D. Grant, C. Hardy, C. Oswick, & L. Putnam (Eds.), *The SAGE handbook of organizational discourse* (pp. 105–127). SAGE Publications. https://doi.org/10.4135/9781848608122
Palmer, I., & Dunford, R. (1996). Conflicting uses of metaphors: Reconceptualizing their use in the field of organizational change. *Academy of Management Review, 21*(3), 691–717.
Perren, L., & Atkin, R. (1997). Owner-manager's discourse: The metaphors-in-use. *Journal of Applied Management Studies, 6*(1), 47–61.
Potter, J. (1996). Representing reality: Discourse, rhetoric and social construction. Sage.
Pragglejaz Group. (2007). MIP: A method for identifying metaphorically used words in discourse. *Metaphor and Symbol, 22*(1), 1–39.
Putnam, L. L., Phillips, N., & Chapman, P. (1996). Metaphors of communication and organizations. In S. R. Clegg & W. R. Nord (Eds.), *Handbook of organization studies* (pp. 375–408). Sage.
Semino, E. (2008). *Metaphor in discourse*. Cambridge University Press.
Smith, R. C., & Eisenberg, E. M. (1987). Conflict at Disneyland: A root-metaphor analysis. *Communications Monographs, 54*(4), 367–380.

Smith, T. H. (2005). Metaphors for navigating negotiations. *Negotiation Journal.* https://doi.org/10.1111/j.0748-4526.2005.00068.x

Steen, G. (2009). Deliberate metaphor affords conscious metaphorical cognition. *Cognitive Semiotics, 5*(1–2), 179–197.

Steen, G. J. (2010). Researching and applying metaphor. *Toegepaste Taalwetenschap in Artikelen (Articles in Applied Linguistics), 83*(1), 91–102.

Steen, G. J., Dorst, A. G., Herrmann, J. B., Kaal, A. A., & Krennmayr, T. (2010). *Metaphor in usage.* De Gruyter.

Vignone, M. J. (2012). Family, buildings and war: Organizational conceptual metaphors. *OD Practitioner, 44*(1), 34–37.

Wittink, J. (2011). Reliable metaphor analysis in organizational research. In *Conference Proceedings from Conference on Organizational Knowledge and Learning Capabilities.*

CHAPTER 4

"The Leadership Team Don't Want to Lead": Using In Situ Categorisations of Leadership and Leader Identity to Do Things in Workplace Activity

Introduction

Despite the amount of ink that has flowed on the subject of leadership, Alvesson and Sveningsson's (2003: 359) observation that "there is considerable discontent with what has been accomplished and it can be argued that we still do not understand leadership particularly well" is still valid 20 years later. Part of this discontent with leadership research could be attributed to the methodological limitations of research which has placed a reliance on questionnaires, surveys, and interviews carried out in research contexts removed from the hurly-burly of actual workplace practice. In order to provide insights into how people understand leadership, data gleaned from such research venues is then often decontextualised, coded, and aggregated out in order to produce grand, catch-all definitions of leadership. Little, if any, research has focused on organisational players as they define what leadership is as part of in situ *everyday workplace practice* and as they deploy the concept to make sense of the organisational environment. Nor have researchers sought to analyse what actions are achieved by defining leadership in one way rather than another. In response to the discontent with leadership research, some researchers (e.g. Fairhurst & Connaughton, 2014; Schnurr & Schroeder, 2019; Tourish,

E. Darics and J. Clifton, *Organisation, Communication and Language*, New Perspectives in Organizational Communication,
https://doi.org/10.1007/978-3-031-30199-5_4

2014) are beginning to argue that taking the linguistic turn in organisational research more seriously might be one way out of the current malaise (see Clifton, Larsson, et al., 2020; Clifton, Schnurr et al., 2020; Larsson, 2016; Larsson & Meier, 2023; Schnurr & Schroeder, 2019; for excellent and recent overviews of this body of research). More specifically, since Gail Fairhurst's (2007) seminal work, researchers taking a discursive approach to leadership are becoming increasingly vociferous. Simply put, considering that talk is action, the aim of discursive leadership research is to capture the doing of leadership as in situ social practice through an analysis of the "micro" practices of talk. In order to make visible the discursive resources through which leadership is achieved, researchers have used various methodologies such as sociolinguistics (Schnurr & Chan, 2011), discourse analysis (Wodak et al., 2011), positioning theory (Clifton, 2018), computer-mediated discourse analysis (Darics, 2020), and so on.

Despite this panoply of approaches, the common ground to such research is the centrality of the analyses of transcripts of naturally occurring interaction through which leadership is said to be achieved. However, to date, such research has concentrated on how leadership is achieved as in situ social practice and has tended to overlook the way in which organisational players' understandings of leadership are constructed in talk. Yet, as Alvesson and Spicer (2011: 4–5) suggest, leadership should be considered not only in terms of practice but also in terms of how people make sense of the world. This, therefore, "involves understanding leadership in terms of how people doing leadership – both leaders and followers – attribute meaning and significance to a whole variety of actions and activities in the workplace. It involves thinking about how some activities are labelled 'leadership' while others are not".

Taking a broadly discursive approach to leadership, in this chapter, we use membership categorisation analysis (MCA) as a method to analyse transcripts of naturally occurring workplace interaction in which the notion of leadership is discussed. Further, we note that if the notion of leadership is discussed in the workplace, it is done so for a reason. Therefore, it is important not only to consider how organisational players define leadership but also to consider what the action of defining leadership in a particular way "does"—something that is rare in leadership research.

More specifically, in order to show how organisational players make sense of what is going on in the organisation and act on it by defining what leadership is, we analyse transcripts of a meeting between Amy,

Kira, and Judith in which they discuss raising awareness of the hospice by including the profile of the leadership team in the local press. Thus, the analyses explicate[1] the participants' in situ category work in and through which they construct *their* version of leadership. Moreover, the category work they do is social action. In other words, it is not only in and through such category work that they make sense of the organisational environment but also through such talk that they act on the organisational landscape and, in this case, attempt to influence the formal leaders of the hospice to take a particular course of action. The exploitation of this data is fairly unique in leadership research because it shows the in situ defining of the "just whatness" of leadership as a member's[2] issue. This is significant since the use of other research methods such as questionnaires, surveys, and interviews invites post hoc reflection on leadership and as such they are one step removed from actual practice. This is because the reflective nature of interviews, surveys, or questionnaires may involve post hoc accounting practices that seek to show the respondent in the best possible light, and which are not therefore direct observations of what actually happens in the workplace. Consequently, it may be that research interviews are recycling existing discourses of leadership that are designed to render the interviewee more leader-like and/or to please the researcher (Alvesson & Sveningsson, 2003). Consequently, other than underlining the popularity of certain discourses of leadership, such interviews may offer few insights into the "just whatness" of leadership. Conversely, through analysing naturally occurring talk in which the notion of leadership is discussed and acted upon, we may be able to obtain fresh insights into the "just whatness" of leadership from the emic perspective of the participants. We may also be able to offer insights into what defining leadership in one way rather than another is designed to achieve.

The chapter is structured as follows. First, we provide a brief overview of the literature relating to leadership from a communicative perspective. We next introduce the reader to MCA, after which we provide fine-grained analyses of the meeting between Amy, Kira, and Judith. Judith is not a member of the fundraising team but the head nurse in the actual

[1] Explicate refers to an unfolding of understanding through closer analysis. It thus eschews recourse to extra-textual notions of causality which are inherent in explanations of phenomena.

[2] A term used in ethnomethodology and conversation analysis to signify a social actor.

hospice. We close the chapter with a discussion of what MCA can offer leadership scholars and practitioners.

Leadership: A Communicative Perspective

It is far beyond the scope of this chapter to provide a detailed review of leadership research—for this we recommend that you have a look at some of the numerous monographs (e.g. Grint, 2010), edited volumes (e.g. Storey et al., 2016), or review articles in journals (e.g. Parry & Bryman, 2013). For the purposes of this chapter, we focus on the relation between language and leadership. Much leadership research, especially that designed for practitioners, has adopted a realist position that treats language as an asocial conduit for communication of "truths" (and "untruths") about leadership. Ontologically speaking, leadership is considered to be a phenomenon that is "out there somewhere" which can be "tamed", identified, measured, and perhaps replicated if one follows the advice of management gurus. In order to make tangible the "just whatness" of leadership, much classic work on leadership has relied on the use of questionnaires and surveys, and has mainly been based on quantitative analyses of large amounts of data (e.g. the classic Ohio State leadership studies [Stodgill, 1950]). However, this approach has led to a proliferation of different definitions of leadership which have little in common other than that they are related to influence in some way (Yukl, 1989). Moreover, as Bass (1990: 11) once famously noted, there are "almost as many different definitions of leadership as there are people who have attempted to define the concept". If Bass is right, then many of these definitions of leadership are either simply wrong or perhaps there are several context-bound definitions of leadership that are possible. However, if leadership is context-bound and contingent on circumstance, the question remains: which of these definitions, even if partial, are "right" and which are "wrong". Given these difficulties, and the proliferation of (sometimes contradictory) definitions of what leadership is, it is not surprising that some leadership scholars are doubtful as to what the combined efforts of leadership researchers actually offer (Alvesson & Sveningsson, 2003; Tourish, 2015). However, if we shift focus to a social constructionist approach in which language constructs, rather than reflects, versions of the world, then descriptions, accounts, and explanations of leadership, rather than being external and prior to language, are located in context-bound human practice and constructed as people communicate. Such an approach to language is thus axiomatic to the linguistic turn in organisational research whereby language use defines, rather than reflects, what we know and how we know it, and so this use produces the objects of which we speak (cf. Chapter 1). Consequently, if we take the linguistic turn in organisational research seriously, it becomes difficult to talk of one unitary reality that is out there somewhere. Rather, there are multiple context-bound versions of leadership that are in constant flux and constantly being constituted and reconstituted as people communicate. From this perspective, the "just whatness" of leadership is constituted in one way rather than another as people talk it, write it, and argue it as part of in situ social practice.

Some key researchers within the field of leadership research are arguing that a way out of this impasse is to take the linguistic turn in organisational/leadership research more seriously (see, e.g., Fairhurst & Connaughton, 2014; Schnurr & Schroeder, 2019; Tourish, 2014). From such a perspective, "leadership is cast as attributional, context dependent, and grounded in social construction processes such as language games and discourse" (Fairhurst & Connaughton, 2014: 17). This implies that we can profitably approach leadership by focusing on the way in which members construct versions of what leadership is as part of their in situ social practice—something that Kelly (2008) argues is rarely considered by researchers, though see, for example, Clifton, Schnurr et al. (2020). The upshot of this, to paraphrase Alvesson and Spicer (2011: 4–5), is that in order to locate leadership, it is necessary to investigate emic in situ understandings of it as people attribute meaning and significance to a whole variety of actions and activities in the workplace that are categorised as leadership. The "just whatness" of leadership, therefore, is necessarily context-bound and ephemeral. Moreover, since it can always be constructed differently in different contexts, it is always open to contestation. Yet, despite this transient nature, it is important to note that constructing a version of leadership is a social act that is not anodyne: constructing the "just whatness" of leadership always does things. In other words, constructing leadership one way rather than another enacts the organisational landscape in a particular way and so promotes, or discourages, certain ways of looking at, and acting in, the world.

In order to make visible and thus analysable the in situ construction of the "just whatness" of leadership and to investigate what action such social practice achieves, we take a discursive approach to leadership. Since Gail Fairhurst's (2007) seminal monograph, discursive approaches to leadership have been undergoing a surge of popularity. Adopting various methods such as critical discourse analysis, conversation analysis, sociolinguistics, and so on, researchers taking a discursive approach to leadership seek to reveal the doing of leadership as in situ action. As Schnurr and Schroeder (2019: 2) put it, discursive leadership "largely focuses on analysing the specific discursive processes through which leadership is accomplished at the micro level of interaction – with the aim of gaining a better understanding of the everyday practices of talk that constitute leadership". While it is fair to say that such work has provided considerable insight into the doing of leadership as situated practice, it has often concentrated on talk that does leadership and overlooked the analysis of the in situ practice of talking about leadership. Therefore, using MCA as a method, in this chapter, we seek to build on prior discursive work on leadership and to add to it by using MCA to investigate how talk about leadership enacts a particular version of it, and how this is an integral part of social action.

Method: Membership Categorisation Analysis (MCA)

Leaders and what they do (leadership) lend themselves to analysis using MCA. This is because MCA seeks to reveal members' practical sociological reasoning as they make sense of their social world through categorising people and defining the predicates (i.e. expectable features, such as beliefs, character traits, behaviours) associated with a particular category/identity (Whittle & Mueller, 2022). In short, as Fitzgerald et al. (2009: 47) succinctly put it, MCA investigates "members' methodical practices in describing the world and displaying their understanding of the world and of the commonsense routine workings of society". Thus, in relation to leadership, MCA provides an analytical tool through which you can make visible, and thus analysable, the way in which members talk into being categories, such as leader, and attribute morally bound predicates to them defining what a leader should and shouldn't do (i.e. defining leadership).

While Harvey Sacks is perhaps most widely known as one of the key players in the development of conversation analysis (see Chapter 7), he also had an interest in considering how social categories are used to describe people and so account for actions and make sense of the world. In his seminal article on categories, the so-called The baby cried. The mommy picked it up paper, Sacks (1986) describes how it is that a reader of the opening sentences of a child's story understands that it is the mother of the infant who picks it up. This is because, as Sacks explains, the world is understood in terms of membership categorisation devices (MCDs) such as "family", in which there are certain categories that commonsensically "go together" such as mother/baby. Each category in the device has a set of category-bound features, i.e. those which are formulated, either explicitly or implicitly, as accompanying some category. Babies, for example, have the category-bound feature of crying. Moreover, Sacks (1972) argues that these categories exist in standardised relational pairs (SRPs) such as mother/baby. Each part of these pairs has a series of responsibilities and obligations vis-à-vis the other so that, for example, the mother of a baby has the moral obligation to pick up the baby when it cries. Thus, it is through such category work that a reader understands that it is *the* mother of *the* baby who picks it up.

However, Sacks never developed his interest in categories into a fully fledged method. After his untimely death in a motor accident in 1975, other researchers (e.g. Fitzgerald & Housley, (eds.) 2015; Hester & Eglin, 1997a; Jayyusi, 1984; Lepper, 2000) developed Sacks' interest in categorisation and focused on the doing of categorisation as situated practical action. However, despite the development of categorisation after Sacks' death, arguably, it is still not a fully developed method; rather, it is a "a collection of observations and an analytical mentality towards observing the ways and methods people orient [to], invoke and negotiate social category based knowledge when engaged in social action" (Housley & Fitzgerald, 2015: 6). Consequently, as Silverman (2012) suggests, at one end of the continuum there is a strong form of MCA, as argued for by researchers such as Hester and Eglin (1997b), which emphasises the inter-relatedness of sequence and category. And, at the other end of the continuum, we can see researchers who are primarily interested in category rather than sequence, and who use MCA as an empirically tractable method for studying members', rather than analysts', categories (Stokoe, 2012: 278).

Despite the existence of strong and weak forms, in a nutshell, MCA is about "how identity is done, managed, achieved and negotiated in situ" (Housley & Fitzgerald, 2015: 2). Such an approach emphasises the doing of categorisation and the *process* of evoking and making relevant to the interaction social categories which describe people, events, institutions, and so on and which *are used to do things* such as accounting for actions, blaming, justifying, and otherwise making sense of the world. Category use is thus context-bound: it is the context which provides for the relevance of the use of any one feature of the category, and it is in terms of the action that is being accomplished that this feature is accountably invoked. Categories are therefore dynamic, fluid, changeable, and open to contestation. Moreover, because categories are occasioned to perform different actions, they are "continually developed, clarified, made accountable, and even retrospectively modified within any unfolding interaction" (Housley & Fitzgerald, 2015: 14).

Furthermore, categories are specifically moral (Jayyusi, 1984). This is because they are organised so that "certain category predicates – such as activities, attributes, rights, responsibilities or knowledge-claims – are viewed as 'properly' associated with particular categories" (Whittle et al., 2015: 379). Failure to display predicates/category-bound features that are enacted as being associated with a particular category is thus a moral issue which can provoke blame, sanction, and criticism: mothers, at the risk of being categorised as poor mothers, have a moral obligation to pick up their crying babies. Fulfilment of moral obligations associated with certain categories and/or displays of certain predicates (i.e. characteristics, thoughts, beliefs, ways of being, etc. associated with a category) become criteria for the incumbency of a certain identity. Therefore, for a person to be occasioned as a leader, mother, police officer, or whatever, they must display that they have the necessary credentials of incumbency (Jayyusi, 1984: 38) that allow them to be constituted "as a good X, which is itself central to the notion of being a genuine X" (Jayyusi, 1984: 44).

To date, with a few noticeable exceptions such as Fairhurst (2007), Larsson and Lundholm (2013), and Whittle et al. (2015), MCA has been little used within leadership research. In these papers, the activity the participants are involved in is not explicitly oriented to as leadership in action by the participants, nor is leader i~ per se specifically oriented to. Rather, etic researcher-driven understandings of leadership are used to interpret the category work that is going on when leadership, as defined by the researcher, is enacted. However, other papers take a more emic approach to the construction of leader identity and they have used MCA to analyse how members' in situ category work talks into being different versions of leadership in research interviews (Clifton & Dai, 2020) and in leadership guru celebrity interviews (Clifton, Schnurr et al., 2020). Building on this work, in this chapter, we focus on the category work that is done by organisational players as they explicitly invoke the category "leader", attribute predicates to incumbents of this category, and use this category work to do something: notably, hold the leadership team at the hospice morally accountable for not fulfilling certain duties, and to account for action which seeks to remedy this situation.

Analysis

The transcripts on which the analyses in this chapter are based are taken from a "hospice awareness meeting" between Amy, Kira, and Judith (cf. Chapter 5, which also uses transcripts of this meeting). During this meeting, they discuss ways of raising the profile of the hospice, and after about 20 minutes, Amy introduces the topic of "people profiles" (i.e. profiles of members of the organisation which they want to put in the local press) and whether the profiles should be those of the nurses and staff or the leaders. We analyse one of these episodes of talk in which the question of whose profile should be in the paper is specifically linked to leadership.

Extract 4.1: What Is a Leader?

In Extract 4.1, while discussing whose profile should go in the press, the participants at the meeting set up an MCD "profiles to go in the press". This category device has two categories within it: leaders and nurses. As the talk progresses, the predicates of the categories of nurses and leaders are defined and these become criteria for incumbency of the category "profile to go in the press". It is, therefore, through the in situ practical action of deciding which profile should go in the press that the category leader is talked into being.

Extract 4.1

1.	Judith	it'd nice to have one of the er: nurse's profiles because I
2.		think (.) that people in the community=those are the ones perhaps=
3.		=although they are hands on they're the ones they might
4.		see as the team that dealt with whoever it was that
5.	Amy	.hh yeah er I mean yeah for me I don't think that I think that
6.		the leaders=
7.	Kira	=Diana I mean the centre she she as the centre=anyone else
8.		like-not lower down but in a different department they only
9.		really represent one part of what happens in the centre so it makes

(continued)

(continued)

10.		sense for Diana to (.) be the profile which then kinda says I
11.		work in the centre
12.		Judith I suppose there are so many facets to it I suppose
13.	Kira	yeah
14.	Amy	for me it's like (.) for me it works that the leaders go on the
15.		hospice awareness because they're the people you come to with your
16.		complaints [with your what is going on in the hospice in the
17.	?	[yeah
18.		future they should know er with the fact that they're the leaders
19.		(.) where you come to going with the actual nurses who deliver
20.		is when you do your newsletter a day in the life of one
21.		of our nurses [and you do a much more you know I wake up at
22.	?	[yeah
23.	Amy	seven in the morning I'm very nervous or actually I really love
24.		what I do or actually very upsetting today because I bla bla
25.		and that's goes much more into a newsletter [it's more you know
26.	?	[uhum
27.		tangible it's more you know a quote is more (.8) I dunno I think it is a
28.		leadership thing so I think it's interesting that we don't have that
29.	Judith	and if you're raising awareness you're almost letting people
30.		understand what structure is how it works
31.	Amy	yeah and you're [in the paper
32.	Judith	[nurses the nurses here all know that

In line 1, Judith takes a turn in which she proposes that they should put a nurse's profile in the press because they are "in the community", "hands-on", and the ones that might be seen "as the team that dealt with whoever". This, therefore, does category work that sets up a category of "nurses" with three predicates: being in the community, being hands-on, and being perceived as those who deal with the patients. However, in line 5, Amy disagrees with this category work and proposes that the leaders' profiles should be in the press. Significantly, then, it is Amy, not us as researchers, who makes the categorisation of "leader" relevant to the interaction. Thus, two categories are established that drive the forthcoming debate: leaders and nurses. Moreover, these categories are constituted as opposing ones within the locally constituted MCD of "profiles to go in the press".

In line 7, Kira latches on to Amy's turn in progress to introduce the topic of Diana, who is ascribed the incumbency of the category of "leader". More specifically, her identity is conflated with the centre (line 7: "she as the centre"), and Kira proposes that, on account of her profile (as a leader), she should be in the press because anyone lower down only represents part of the organisation. Leaders, then, are talked into being with the predicate of being/representing the organisation, and this is why their profile should be in the press. In line 14, Amy affiliates with this assessment and continues her work of categorising the leader and accounting for her suggestion that the leaders' profiles should be in the hospice awareness article in the press. This category work is explicitly accounted for in terms of leadership (line 18: "the fact they're leaders", and line 27: "it's a leadership thing"), and leaders are occasioned as having the predicates of being the people "you come to with your complaints" and having knowledge of "what is going on in the hospice in the future" (lines 15 and 16). Significantly, this knowledge is explicitly treated as a moral issue and something the leader *should* have (line 18) but which they "don't have" (line 28). Further, the predicates attached to the category "leader" are set up in opposition to the category "nurses" who "deliver". Consequently, as Amy argues, nurses as a category should be in a newsletter which is much more, to gloss line 20 and following, "a day in the life of". In short, the "just whatness" of leadership is thus constructed so that it "does something"—in this case accounting for a suggestion to place profiles in the press.

To sum up, in this extract, Amy, Kira, and Judith set up an MCD—"profiles that should be in the press". There are two opposing candidate categories that could go in the press: nurses and leaders. The leaders have the category-bound predicates of representing or even being the centre, being someone to turn to if you have a complaint, and of having knowledge of what is going on in the hospice. Nurses are attributed the predicate of being able to "deliver". The leaders have the requisite credentials of incumbency so their profiles should be in the press. The nurses, on the other hand, have the credentials of incumbency to be in a newsletter. Thus, we demonstrate how the "just whatness" of leadership is constructed in the local context of a meeting to achieve a particular end, i.e. that of deciding whose profile should appear in the press.

Extract 4.2: Are the Hospice's Leaders Really Leaders?

Having set up two opposing categories whose profiles are being considered for inclusion in the press, Amy, Kira, and Judith go on to consider whether the current leadership team have the credentials of incumbency that enable them to be incumbent of the category "leader" that has been made relevant in the prior talk.

Extract 4.2

33.	Amy	yeah
34.	Judith	[but ( )
35.	Amy	[and who-who they're for actually you don't want someone
36.		to call your nurse you want that person to call Pete if they've
37.		got an issue with the paper or [or something to do with the inpatients
38.	?	[yeah
39.	Amy	centre don't actually want to put your people in the frontline
40.		I don't think in this particular situation I didn't think of that yesterday
41.	Judith	no I didn't either but now I'm thinking actually are they equipped
42.		to deal with the public backlash
43.	Amy	yeah
44.	Judith	of the sort=if there is any backlash
45.	Amy	backlash or just questions oh look my gran's got cancer and I didn't
46.		know about [it (.) don't want to call for the nurse you want to call
47.	?	[yeah
48.		for Pete or Jay or=and maybe we could go back and say that and
49.		maybe that would be a good argument

In line 33 and following, Amy continues the oppositional categorisation of leaders and nurses within the MCD "profile that is suitable to go in the press". Nurses are occasioned as being people who "you don't want someone to call" (line 35) and who you don't want to put in the frontline (line 39) and so two more predicates are added to the list relevant to the category "nurse"—implicitly, then, leaders are occasioned as having the predicates that you want someone to call and who you want to put in the frontline. Pete, considering the prior talk is occasioned as incumbent of the category leader, is implicitly attributed leader identity. This is because he has the predicate of being "someone you want to call … if they've got an issue with the paper or something to do with the inpatients" (lines 36 and 37). Significantly here, Amy sets up a moral category. This is because the predicates of the category of "leader" are established in terms of what "you" want or don't want.

In lines 41 and 42, Judith questions whether they (i.e. the leaders at the hospice) "actually are they equipped to deal with the public backlash" and thus whether they actually have the credentials to be incumbent of the category of "leader", as talked into being by the participants so far. This sets up a moral discrepancy (Housley, 2002) between what is morally expected of the leaders and what the leaders in the hospice are able to do.

Amy (line 45) aligns with this category work and adds to it by doubting whether the hospice's leaders are able to deal with questions like "oh look my gran's got cancer and I didn't know about it". Amy then returns to her previous category work and continues to set up the category of "nurse" in opposition to that of "leader" (line 46: "don't want to call for the nurse you want to call for Jill or Pete"). Jill and Pete are, therefore, ascribed incumbency to the category of "leader", and the potential moral discrepancy of the hospice's leaders not being able to deal with the backlash or questions is, temporarily at least, left in suspension.

In short, the participants continue setting up leaders and nurses as oppositional categories within the MCD "profiles to go in the press". The category of "leader" is occasioned as one that could go in the press, whereas nurses are not. However, the potential discrepancy between the criteria of incumbency of the category of "leader" and the actual predicates linked to the "leaders" of the hospice has been raised, though at this point it is not particularly developed.

Extract 4.3: Acting on the Category Work

Having made relevant the category of "leader" and raised doubts as to whether the hospice's leaders have the requisite predicates to be incumbent of this category, Amy, Kira, and Judith now draw out the practical consequences of such categorisation work. Thus, the way in which leaders are categorised paves the way, and accounts, for action.

Extract 4.3

48.	Amy	for Pete or Jill or=and maybe we could go back and say that and
49.		maybe that would be a good argument
50.	?	to have another
51.	Amy	and say we really want to do all you're saying but we want
52.		the leaders in there because you can answer the bigger questions
53.		if they come up and it can be some=what my mum's been diagnosed
54.	Judith	yeah
55.	Amy	can I speak to Diana or you know what I mean not-not the
56.		receptionist [or the volunteer but actually someone who can do
57.	?	[ehum
58.		something about it
59.	Judith	yeah
60.	Kira	did he respond to your email at all
61.	Amy	no he's busy doubt he looks at his emails [all the time d'you we
62.		[yeah

(continued)

(continued)

63.		could=I-I could send an email to the leaders if you like we've
64.		got a leadership next Tuesday↑ meeting we could

In line 48, Amy suggests that maybe they could go back to the leadership team, with whom they had had a meeting the previous day, and present them with a new argument, i.e. that the leaders' profiles, not the nurses', should be in the press because they are the ones who "can answer the bigger questions if they come up" (line 52). Thus, the category work that Amy, Kira, and Judith have done provides grounds for action. In other words, having ascribed predicates to the category of "leader", those incumbent of this category (i.e. Pete, Jill, Diana, and others in the leadership team) have the moral obligation to display these predicates. Moreover, since they should have these predicates, they are morally bound to be the ones, rather than the nurses, to appear in the press.

Amy then exemplifies this with a short hypothetical story of a potential incident in which somebody asks to speak to Diana because their mum has been diagnosed with cancer. Diana is thus incumbent of the category of "leader" and in this short story, she is occasioned as somebody who "can do something about it" (line 56). The category of "leader", of which Diana is incumbent, is also talked into being as oppositional to the category of "volunteer", who implicitly can't do anything about it.

Extract 4.4: Telling the Leaders What to Do

At the end of the prior extract, Amy proposes to send an email to the "leaders". The next 20 lines, in which the participants decide who exactly they are going to send the email to, are not analysed for reasons of space. We rejoin the analysis when Amy defines what they are going to put in the email.

Extract 4.4

84.	Amy	we put in the kinda quotes we wanted them to say
85.	Judith	well I said a little bit about how long have you been
86.		in the hospice what's your role in terms of what it means for you
87.	Amy	shall we write it for them
88.	Judith	yeah I did offer
89.	Amy	why don't you do it and say this is as an example if you as a

(continued)

(continued)

90.		team so you won't be all saying the same thing this is what
91.		we'd be thinking of kinda thing that around then in your own words
92.	Kira	yeah
93.	Judith	well Diana's gonna get hers to me by the end of
94.	Amy	oh okay
95.	Judith	so maybe we can use that
96.	Amy	she might not though because now she's got like her team the
97.		leadership team don't want to lead ((spoken in 'funny voice'))
98.		but then I suggest managed to give myself something in addition
99.		to do is when potentially when Tom comes in to do the thank yous

In line 84, Amy suggests that the content of the email should include the "kinda quotes we wanted them to say". In other words, Amy, Kira, and Judith, who are hierarchically subordinate to the leaders, plan to tell the leaders not only, on account of the previous category work, to put their profiles in the press but also what these profiles should contain. Judith affiliates with this suggestion: she has already suggested that the leaders should include "a little bit about how long have you been in the hospice what's your role in terms of what it means for you" (lines 85–86). Amy then (line 87) suggests: "shall we write it for them". In line 93, Judith says that Diana will get her profile to her by the end of the week and suggests that they use that as an example. Amy negatively assesses this suggestion, arguing that Diana might not give Judith her profile because "now she's got like her team". This is then assessed: "the leadership team don't want to lead". This is uttered in what can only be called "a funny voice", with a variation in tone and pitch that sets it apart from the surrounding talk. This draws attention to the evaluation and perhaps marks it out as slightly humorous, so mitigating the potentially damaging assessment and/or indicating the absurdity of this paradox. The upshot of the prior category work is thus crystallised in this assessment: the de jure leaders are not fulfilling their moral obligations and are failing to provide leadership. This is because, in this instance, leaders are ascribed the predicates of being the people who: "you" want to go to if you have a complaint (line 15); know what is going on in the future (line 15); and can answer the bigger questions and actually do something about it. Consequently, they have the criteria of incumbency so their profile should be in the press. However, since they are not providing the profiles, they are not fulfilling their leadership obligations and are thus held morally accountable for not wanting to lead. The failure to provide their profiles for the paper is thus made sense of through category work which accounts for their reticence to provide the profiles as a lack of leadership. Moreover, as a result of this category work, Amy, Kira, and Judith act (i.e. they draft an email) to influence the "leaders" to fulfil their moral responsibilities and obligations (as defined in the category work) to provide their profiles.

In short, the category work that Amy, Judith, and Kira have enacted is used to account for an attempt to influence the leaders to do something (i.e. to put their profiles in the press). Interestingly, this reverses most traditional work in which leadership is considered to be a process of top-down influence from hierarchical superiors to subordinates in which "leaders drive required change from the top" (Grint, 2010: 4). Yet, in stark contrast to this somewhat conventional, researcher-inspired definition of leadership, the action that the category work of Amy, Kira, and Judith does is to manage their leaders. This aligns with the increasing research interest in post-heroic versions of leadership in which influence can be lateral, bottom-up, as well as top-down (Gronn, 2002: 431). We develop this point in the discussions below.

Observations and Discussions

In the analyses presented in this chapter, we show how the category of leader is talked into being as part of in situ social practice and how this categorisation work paves the way for action. The category of leader is constructed as not only being/representing the organisation (line 7) but also as having the category-bound features of being able to answer and act on the bigger questions (line 51), deal with complaints (line 15), and know what is going on in the future (line 15). Because those to whom the identity of leader has been ascribed are attributed with these category-bound features, their profiles should be in the press. Reticence to have their profiles in the press becomes a moral issue for which they are held accountable: "the leadership team don't want to lead". As such, they are not real and genuine leaders. Moreover, this particular context-bound category work paves the way for action. In an attempt to persuade the leadership team to put their profiles in the paper, Amy, Kira, and Judith will send an email telling them what to do in order to fulfil their morally bound leadership role.

We can see that these findings, therefore, have significant implications for leadership research which, as pointed out in the introduction, has been dominated by approaches which have used surveys, questionnaires, and interviews that solicit definitions of leadership that allow considerable post hoc reflection from respondents and which are removed from actual workplace practice. However, if you take the linguistic turn in organisation studies seriously and investigate the in situ defining of leader identity as context-bound social practice that is designed to "do" something, then a very different picture begins to emerge.

First, then, it is important to note that the categorisation of leader and the predicates that are associated with him/her are specifically designed for the context in which it occurs. In this case, a particular version of leader identity is talked into being and is juxtaposed with that of a nurse and, to a lesser extent, a volunteer. Thus, we claim that the "just whatness" of leadership is not something that exists as a context-free, pre-discursive phenomenon that is out there somewhere; rather, it is necessarily a context-bound and situated achievement. It would be difficult to imagine the definition of leadership as talked into being by Amy, Kira, and Judith being transferable to other situations outside of the hospice. Would, for example, the leaders (e.g. Eisenhower, Carnegie, Kennedy, etc.) typified in Zaleznik's (1977/2004) classic paper on the difference between managers and leaders be talked into being in terms of the moral responsibility of having their profiles in the papers, or set up in contrast to the category of "nurse"? Thus, rather than having a catch-all definition of leadership that is perhaps so vague that it means all things to all people (Bresnen, 1995), in the to-and-fro of everyday workplace activity there is more likely to be a kaleidoscope of ephemeral definitions of leadership that are variously invoked according to the context in which they emerge, and according to what these definitions are designed to achieve.

The upshot of this is that as well as seeking out definitions of what leadership is, or leaders are, you could also focus your attention on what definitions of leadership "do". In this case, the definition of leadership that Amy, Judith, and Kira talk into being is used to decide whose profile should go in the press, hold the leaders at the hospice morally accountable for a lack of leadership ("the leadership team don't want to lead"), and provide a springboard for action. Significantly, the future action involves sending the leadership team an email in an attempt to persuade them to put their profiles in the press. Interestingly, while leadership is classically defined in heroic terms as the doing of top-down influence, our analyses reveal that it is the hierarchical subordinates who set about influencing the leadership team. Thus, our analyses align with the surge of interest in post-heroic forms of leadership in which leadership is a shared, distributed, or plural phenomenon and influence can be not only top-down as traditionally conceived but also bottom-up or lateral (Gronn, 2002).

Furthermore, taking a more context-bound and discursive approach to leadership aligns with the interests of critical leadership scholars who, inter alia, seek to challenge the traditional dichotomous and asymmetrical view of leaders and followers in which followers are conceived of as agentless social actors who are waiting to be led and influenced by hierarchically superior leaders (Collinson, 2018). Critical leadership scholars argue that such a dichotomous view of leadership is too simplistic and too ideologically convenient to be taken seriously and that followers (conceived of as subordinates) are frequently proactive agents. Indeed, in the analyses presented in this chapter, it is clear that the "followers" (subordinates) are active in challenging the leaders (hierarchical superiors). Paradoxically, then, these analyses turn traditional heroic leadership research on its head and show that it is the subordinates who set out to do the leading by influencing their superiors to take a particular course of action. Arguing that it is the followers who do the leading is, of course, oxymoronic and calls into question the whole dichotomy of leader and follower based on top-down influence and hierarchical position.

Such a perspective on leadership also has an impact on practice. Most work on leadership at the popular end of the market that is designed for leadership training adopts a heroic approach in which leaders are distinct from followers and the leader's superiority over the subordinate/followers is rarely called into question (Tourish et al., 2010). This is exemplified by the sales "blurb" on the numerous leadership trainers' and consultants' websites in which they sell their programmes on the grounds that leaders are different from, and superior to, subordinates. For example, on his webpages, Tony Robbins, a contemporary and popular management/leadership guru, defines leadership as an ability "to communicate a clear vision and then unite your team around that vision".[3] This may or may not be true, yet implicitly it differentiates leaders from the "team" (read: followers) who are prepared to accept "their leader's" vision. This kind of

[3] https://www.tonyrobbins.com/what-is-leadership.

popular conception of leadership prevalent in leadership training, therefore, consolidates and promotes the notion of the heroic leader which is equated with hierarchical position. Yet, if, as the analyses in this chapter indicate, subordinates set out to manage (failing) leaders by telling them what to do, and if (popular) conceptions of leaders as those wielding top-down influence, as often claimed, is not quite as clear-cut as it would seem, then leaders (as hierarchic superiors) should be wary of buying uncritically into leadership training in which they are cast as the ones who heroically set direction, create vision, empower their followers to achieve this vision, and so on. Indeed, buying wholeheartedly into such top-down versions of leadership may well be favourable to the development of hubris and excessive ego that Tourish (2013), for example, attributes to leadership failures in such cases as the collapse of Enron or the banking crisis of 2008. Perhaps a way around this is for leadership trainers to pay less attention to grand "theories" of leadership and more to the in situ enactment of leadership (cf. Clifton, 2006).

It also means that the leaders should be aware of how their actions are perceived by their subordinates. In other words, hierarchical position is not enough to ensure that subordinates view the management as leaders. Rather, leader identity, as with any other category, is always in a state of flux and can always be constructed otherwise. In this case, the leadership team is held morally accountable for not fulfilling their obligations. Paradoxically, the leadership team don't lead, and therefore, the leadership of the hospice is talked into being as failing. An awareness of the situated construction of the "just whatness" of leadership, and the way in which these constructions can counter heroic notions of leadership promoted by the leadership training industry, may then be a useful tool for managers to have. It may also be an antidote to the hubris and arrogance that such heroic notions of leadership may promote and which, as Tourish et al. (2010) point out, may have a negative influence on the organisational environment.

Membership Categorisation Analysis as a Method

As argued above, taking a linguistic, and more specifically MCA, approach to analysis of organisations has the ability to provide critical insights that other methods may not be able to provide. MCA can help us sidestep mainstream understandings of organisational phenomena, in this case leadership, and see them from a more critical angle. To do this, first, locate stretches of talk that you find interesting, paying particular attention to how the participants "describe" themselves and others. What devices are used to group these categories? What predicates are attributed to these categories? What rights and obligations are attributed to these categories and how are the categories set up in relation to each other? This category work is shot through with morality (who *should* do what to whom), so pay particular attention to any moral judgements that are made. Also, consider what actions such category work achieves.

In the particular example we have showcased in this chapter, we were particularly interested in leader identity. This is because the participants themselves made the category of "leader" relevant to the interaction. The big advantage of this is that by avoiding starting with researcher-driven definitions of leaders and leadership, we may be able to get to the way in which organisational players use categories to build a sense of what their organisation is for them. It allows us, in a way, to listen to the voices of the organisational players, without being cluttered by a priori research-driven theories of who leaders are or what leadership should be. In this case, such an approach reveals the category work that the organisational players do and it shows them, the subordinates, doing the leading in the face of a management team that doesn't want to lead. This, to some extent, turns popularised conceptions of leadership, in which influence is top-down, on their head and shows the potential of MCA for critical inquiry.

Conclusions

In conclusion, it can be seen that a linguistic approach to the analysis of leadership has the ability to reveal the actual in situ practices of categorising people as leaders or events as leadership. The findings of this chapter present a serious challenge to prior leadership research which has had a predilection for studies based on interviews and surveys and which, because of the distance from the actual practices of categorising something as leadership or somebody as a leader, has run the risk that Alvesson and Sveningsson (2003) pointed out 20 years ago of merely obtaining recycled versions of popular grand theories of leadership. Contrary to this, the findings of this chapter reveal that leadership and leader identity as negotiated in the context of the hospice are something quite banal and context-bound (i.e. whose profile goes in the newspaper). However, significantly, wanting to place a profile in the newspaper is seen as a moral action and failure to do so as a failure in leadership. Further, considering the in situ category work of categorising something as leadership, or someone as a leader, allows the researcher to make tangible the social action that this achieves, which in this case is criticising. Moreover, in order to redress the perceived lack of leadership from the leadership team, it is the subordinates who take action to incite the leadership team to fulfil their perceived responsibilities. Significantly, this turns classic heroic leadership theories, which often equate leader identity and leadership with hierarchic position, on their head and so seriously challenges the relevance of these theories to members' practice. Taking the linguistic turn seriously in your research and considering the actual workplace practices in which organisational phenomena, such as leadership, are invoked as a member's phenomenon, rather than a researcher's phenomenon, is a prime way of making tangible emic orientations to such phenomena. As demonstrated in this chapter, starting as it were "bottom-up" from in situ social practice, rather than as it were "top-down" from theory, enables you to look at phenomena of interest to scholars but through a new lens. This may give fresh insights which, as in this case, may challenge accepted thinking on the subject and allow for some kind of critical reappraisal of existing theories.

References

Alvesson, M., & Spicer, A (2011). Introduction. In M. Alvesson & A. Spicer (Eds.), *Metaphors we lead by. Understanding leadership in the real world* (pp. 1–8). Routledge.

Alvesson, M., & Sveningsson, S. (2003). The great disappearing act: Difficulties in doing "leadership." *The Leadership Quarterly, 14*(3), 359–381.

Bass, B. (1990). *Bass and Stodgill's handbook of leadership* (3rd ed.) The Free Press.

Bresnen, M. J. (1995). All things to all people? Perceptions, attributions, and constructions of leadership. *The Leadership Quarterly, 6*(4), 495–513.

Clifton, J. (2006). A conversation analytical approach to business communication: The case of leadership. *The Journal of Business Communication, 43*(3), 202–219.

Clifton, J. (2018). The in situ construction of leader identity in a leader's life story during an alumni talk to MBA students. *Leadership, 14*(6), 622–643.

Clifton, J., & Dai, W. (2020). A discursive analysis of the in situ construction of (Japanese) leadership and leader identity in a research interview. Implications for leadership research. *Leadership, 16*(2), 180–199.

Clifton, J., Larsson, M., & Schnurr, S. (2020). Leadership in interaction. An introduction to the special issue. *Leadership, 16*(5), 511–521.
Clifton, J., Schnurr, S., & Van De Mieroop, D. (2020). *The language of leadership narratives*. Routledge.
Collinson, D. L. (2018). Critical leadership studies: Exploring the dialectics of leadership. In R. Riggio (Ed.), *What's wrong with leadership?* (pp. 260–278). Routledge.
Darics, E. (2020). E-leadership or "how to be boss in instant messaging?" The role of nonverbal communication. *International Journal of Business Communication, 57*(1), 3–29.
Fairhurst, G. (2007). *Discursive leadership: In conversation with leadership psychology*. Sage.
Fairhurst, G., & Connaughton, S. (2014). Leadership: A communicative perspective. *Leadership, 10*(1), 7–35.
Fitzgerald, R., & Housley, W. (Eds.). (2015). *Advances in membership categorisation analysis*. Sage.
Fitzgerald, R., Housley, W., & Butler, C. W. (2009). Omnirelevance and interactional context. *Australian Journal of Communication, 36*(3), 45–64.
Grint, K. (2010). *Leadership: A very short introduction.* Oxford University Press.
Gronn, P. (2002). Distributed leadership as a unit of analysis. *The Leadership Quarterly, 13*(4), 423–451.
Hester, S., & Eglin, P. (Eds.) (1997a). *Culture in action: Studies in membership categorization analysis.* University Press of America.
Hester, S., & Eglin, P. (1997b). Conclusions: Membership categorization analysis and sociology. In S. Hester & P. Eglin (Eds.), *Culture in action: Studies in membership categorization analysis* (pp. 153–163). University Press of America.
Housley, W. (2002). Moral discrepancy and 'fudging the issue' in a radio news interview. *Sociology, 36*(1), 5–21.
Housley, W., & Fitzgerald, R. (2015). Introduction to membership categorisation analysis. In R. Fitzgerald & W. Housley (Eds.), *Advances in membership categorisation analysis* (pp. 1–22). Sage.
Jayyusi, L. (1984). *Categorization and the moral order.* Routledge.
Kelly, S. (2008). Leadership: A categorical mistake? *Human Relations, 61*(6), 763–782.
Larsson, M. (2016). Leadership in interaction. In J. Storey, J. Hartley, J.-L. Denis, P. t' Hart & D. Ulrich (Eds.), *Routledge companion to leadership* (pp. 173–194). Routledge.
Larsson, M., & Lundholm, S. E. (2013). Talking work in a bank: A study of organizing properties of leadership in work interactions. *Human Relations, 66*(8), 1101–1129.

Larsson, M., & Meier, F. (2023). Leadership in interaction. In D. Schedlitzki, M. Larsson, B. Carroll, M. Bligh, & O. Epitropaki (Eds.), *Sage handbook of leadership* (pp. 28–39). Sage.

Lepper, G. (2000). *Categories in text and talk: A practical introduction to categorization analysis*. Sage.

Parry, K., & Bryman, A. (2013). Leadership in organizations. In S. Clegg, C. Hardy, T. Lawrence, & W. Nord (Eds.), *The Sage handbook of organisation studies* (2nd Ed., pp. 447–468). Sage.

Sacks, H. (1972). An initial investigation of the usability of conversational data for doing sociology. In D. Sudnow (Ed.), *Studies in social interaction* (pp. 31–74). Free Press.

Sacks, H. (1986). On the analyzability of stories by children. In J. J. Gumperz & D. Hymes (Eds.), *Directions in sociolinguistics: The ethnography of communication* (pp. 325–345). Basil Blackwell.

Schnurr, S., & Chan, A. (2011). Exploring another side of co-leadership: Negotiating professional identities through face-work in disagreements. *Language in Society, 40*(2), 187–209.

Schnurr, S., & Schroeder, A. (2019). A critical reflection of current trends in discourse analytical research on leadership across disciplines. A call for a more engaging dialogue. *Leadership, 15*(4), 445–460.

Silverman, D. (2012). Beyond armed camps: A response to Stokoe. *Discourse Studies, 14*(3), 329–336.

Stodgill, R. (1950). Leadership, membership and organization. *Psychological Bulletin, 47*, 1–14.

Stokoe, E. (2012). Moving forward with membership categorisation analysis: Methods for systematic analysis. *Discourse Studies, 14*(3), 277–303.

Storey, J., Hartley, J., Davis, J.-L., t'Hart, P. & Ulrich, D. (Eds.) (2016). *The Routledge companion to leadership.* Routledge.

Tourish, D. (2013). *The dark side of transformational leadership: A critical perspective*. Routledge.

Tourish, D. (2014). Leadership, more or less? A processual, communication perspective on the role of agency in leadership theory. *Leadership, 10*(1), 79–98.

Tourish, D. (2015). Some announcements, reaffirming the critical ethos of leadership and what we look for in submissions. *Leadership, 11*(2), 135–141.

Tourish, D., Craig, R., & Amernic, J. (2010). Transformational leadership education and agency perspectives in business school pedagogy: A marriage of inconvenience? *British Journal of Management, 21*(1), 40–59.

Whittle, A., & Mueller, F. (2022). Membership categorisation analysis: Developing awareness of categories and their consequences. In E. Darics (Ed.), *Language awareness in business and the professions* (pp. 183–204). Cambridge University Press.

Whittle, A., Housley, W., Gilchrist, A., Mueller, F., & Lenney, P. (2015). Category predication work, discursive leadership and strategic sense-making. *Human Relations, 68*(3), 377–407.

Wodak, R., Kwon, W., & Clarke, I. (2011). 'Getting people on board': Discursive leadership for consensus building in team meetings. *Discourse & Society, 22*(5), 592–644.

Yukl, G. (1989). Managerial leadership: A review of theory and research. *Journal of Management, 15*(2), 251–289.

Zaleznik, A. (1977/2004). Managers and leaders: Are they different? *Harvard Business Review*, *55*(3), 67–76.

CHAPTER 5

When Organisation Makes No Sense: Rumour and Narratives in the Making

Introduction

As many researchers (e.g. Boje, 2001; Rhodes & Brown, 2005; Weick, 2012) have pointed out, stories[1] are a key site of sense-making in organisations. Once organisational players have a story, a sense of order is imposed on the organisational landscape, and it can be acted upon. Thus, storytelling allows organisational players, to paraphrase Chia (2000: 513), to make sense of the flux of brute aboriginal lived experience that surrounds them and to fix, name, label, and classify it—all intrinsic processes of discursive organisations—so as to construct a (their) version of organisational reality and act upon it. Conversely, without a story to follow, the organisational landscape could easily become a chaotic flux of impressions which provides no direction for action. Moreover, the lack of an official story may give rise to rumours which, as Bordia et al. (2006: 604) argue, "arise from an *informal*, collective sense-making" (italics added).

While rumours have been the attention of significant academic work (e.g. Liff & Wikström, 2021; Michelson & Mouly, 2002; Waddington,

[1] In this chapter, considering the difference between narratives and stories to be more of a researcher's etic distinction than a social actor's emic distinction, we use stories and narratives as synonyms.

E. Darics and J. Clifton, *Organisation, Communication and Language*, New Perspectives in Organizational Communication, https://doi.org/10.1007/978-3-031-30199-5_5

2021), little of this looks at the in situ social practice of "rumouring". Using interactional sociolinguistics as a methodology and working within a narrative as social practice paradigm (De Fina, 2021; De Fina & Georgakopoulou, 2008a, 2008b, 2015; Van De Mieroop et al., 2022), the purpose of this chapter is to analyse the way in which rumours arise as part of everyday workplace practice and to investigate how the storytellers try to make sense of what may or may not be happening in the organisation. Findings indicate that organisational players turn to rumour in the absence of a strong leadership narrative and that rumouring creates an organisational reality in which a divisive "us-and-them" dichotomy is enacted which reduces the field of action. Further, unlike much previous work on sense-making that casts managers as practical authors (Shotter, 1993) or leaders as managers of meaning (Smircich & Morgan, 1982), we focus on the way in which subordinates also manage meaning, through rumouring, in ways that may lead to less than optimal outcomes for the organisation. More specifically, picking up on the previous chapter in which we saw that the different metaphors used talked into being a divided organisation, in this chapter, we see how rumouring also talks into being a divided organisation.

This chapter is structured as follows. First, we outline the literature relating to rumour and organisation. We then explain the approach, namely narrative as social practice and method of analysis, namely interactional sociolinguistics. We then analyse a transcript of talk, which follows on from the meeting between Amy, Kira, and Judith, as discussed in Chapter 4, and in which they try to make sense of what is going on in the organisation by storying it and making sense of the situation. We close the chapter with observations and conclusions.

Literature Review: Rumour

Allport and Postman's seminal (1947) work on the psychology of rumour was the first to take rumour seriously and not dismiss it as idle gossip. Since then rumour has been on the agenda of researchers from various disciplines, such as anthropology, sociology, psychology, and communication. Simply put, rumour relates to communication that passes through unofficial, rather than official, channels of communication in organisation (Michelson & Mouly, 2004: 189). Rumours are, as Rosnow (1991: 488) states, "public communications infused with private hypotheses about how the world works". They have been variously categorised as "pipe dreams" (i.e. wish fulfilment); "bogies" (i.e. rumour based on anxiety); aggressive rumours that seek to damage reputations and do harm; and anticipatory rumours that are often fostered by situations of ambiguity (Michelson & Mouly, 2000). Despite these various ways of categorising rumours, there is consensus among researchers that rumours, while being pervasive in organisations, are particularly present in times of uncertainty in which organisational players try to make sense of what is going on around them (e.g. Balogun, 2007; Bordia et al., 2006; DiFonzo & Bordia, 1988; Michelson & Mouly, 2004; Rosnow, 1991: 488). They are, therefore, said to flourish in periods of organisational change, especially when there is an absence of an official narrative explaining the whys and wherefores of the change or when the information that is offered by the organisation's leadership is treated with scepticism and suspicion (DiFonzo & Bordia, 1988). These doubts and anxieties are magnified if employees believe that these changes may result in redundancies, as in the case of restructuring and downsizing (Bordia et al., 2004). Consequently, rumours often have negative connotations, and the propagation of them is often associated with negative consequences for the organisation, leading to stress, turnover of personnel, and lower productivity and performance (Bordia et al., 2004). As a result, on account of negative connotations attached to rumour, it is often argued that leaders should take steps to manage them and reduce their impact by, for example, involving the employees in change management through participative decision-making and communicating as openly as possible and improving the quality of the information given to employees (DiFonzo & Bordia, 1988). Further, rumours are often considered to be vehicles of fake news (Bondielli & Marcelloni, 2019). However, recognising the polyphony of organisational storytelling, and the existence of *truths* rather than *a single truth*, we would be naive to consider official stories as the truth of the situation and unofficial stories (i.e. rumours) as false and incomplete in some way. Rather, both rumour and officially sanctioned organisational stories are ways of making sense of what is happening: they establish veracity (i.e. a quality or a semblance of being true) for the storytellers.

However, despite recognition of the importance and pervasiveness of rumours within organisations, as various researchers (e.g. Bordia et al., 2006; Michelson & Mouly, 2000) argue, rumour still remains an under-researched phenomenon in organisational studies. Moreover, as Spear and Roper (2016) point out, when research into rumour in organisational settings does exist, it often takes a top-down perspective considering how leaders control the top-down flow of information during organisational change and how they manage rumours. Little research has been carried out into how information in times of change is received by employees. Conversely, focusing on the fundraising team and how their rumouring authors a particular organisational landscape, in this chapter, we move attention away from the leadership team as managers of meaning to focus on how other organisational players, as managers of meaning, may, through rumour, story into being alternative, less flattering, and divisive organisational landscapes. Thus, we assess how rumours are enacted by subordinates—often the forgotten "foot soldiers" in organisational research—rather than how they are considered by "the management".

Further, existing research on rumour is often based on interviews or surveys (see, e.g., Bordia et al., 2006; DiFonzo & Bordia, 1988; Spear & Roper, 2016). Relying on surveys and interviews gives second-order accounts of what people perceive rumours to be and/or to do, but it does not give us access to rumour as it happens in real time. To address this lacuna, we use the transcripts of a meeting between Amy, Kira, and Judith in which they try to make sense of what is going on in the organisation, notably a lack of leadership, as discussed in the previous chapter. They do this by hypothesising about what is going on and negotiating storylines that explain and make sense of the organisation as it appears to them. Analysing rumour as it emerges is especially important from a social constructionist perspective in which making sense is not a question of grasping some underlying organisational reality (or truth); rather, sense-making is about *constructing* an organisational landscape, which provides constraints and resources for organisational players to act within that landscape. This is especially important in times of change because shifts in the way in which the organisational landscape is authored open up, and close down, new possibilities for action and therefore change. To analyse this storying of what is going on, we take a narrative as social practice approach, as discussed below.

Narrative as Social Practice and Interactional Sociolinguistics

Stories, as Georgakopoulou (2011: 190) noted, are "inescapably fundamental in human life, central to the (re)constitution and interpretation of personal, social, and cultural reality". This observation has not been overlooked by organisational scholars who have embraced the narrative turn in organisational studies which Fenton and Langley (2011: 1174) sum up as a move "away from inquiry aimed at establishing universal relationships among abstract concepts and towards the understanding of how human beings make meaning, constructing experience, knowledge, and identity through narrative". While it is beyond the scope of this chapter to provide an in-depth view of narratives in organisational research (see, e.g., Boje, 2001, 2008; Rhodes & Brown, 2005; Vaara et al., 2016), suffice to say that organisational studies, as a discipline, has displayed a strong interest in the use of narrative analysis to investigate issues of concern to organisational scholars such as sense-making, communication, politics and power, learning and change, and identity and identification (Rhodes & Brown, 2005).

In this chapter, we concentrate on stories as devices for sense-making. This is because it is through stories, whether official or unofficial, that people make sense of their experiences, impose order, share values, and establish meaning (Weick, 1995). In short, as Weick (1995: 128) puts it, "when people punctuate their own living into stories, they impose a formal coherence on what is otherwise a flowing soup". Commensurate with this perspective on storytelling, authors such as Shotter (1993) have put forward the idea that managers are practical authors, which is to say that through their sense-making they author a particular version of the organisational landscape. Similarly, Smircich and Morgan (1982) cast leaders as managers of meaning because their role in the organisation is to frame and define "reality" for others. However, stories are about more than "just" making sense—sense-making is also intertwined with action. This is because organisations are not pre-discursive social structures; rather, they are relational landscapes that are continually shifting as organisational players make sense of them and define the constraints and possibilities for their actions as players within such organisational landscapes. Thus, as we argue in this chapter, failure to make sense of the situation and to produce a narrative to account for it leads to a lack of sense and a propensity for inaction rather than action.

In order to investigate the in situ doing of rumour, we take a narrative as social practice approach to analysis. For a recent overview of narratives as social practice see De Fina (2021), and, more specifically, for an overview of research taking a social practice approach to narratives in organisational settings see Van De Mieroop et al. (2022). As De Fina and Georgakopoulou (2008a) point out, conventionally, narratives have mainly been considered in terms of their structure, having a clear beginning, middle, and end, and as coherent monologues of personal experience removed from the context of the storytelling. See, for example, Labov and Waletzky's (1967) conception of narrative structure which has had a profound influence on decades of linguistic narrative research. They discern six elements that usually—but not always—occur in a prototypical narrative, namely: the abstract (a summary of the upcoming story); the orientation (a section orienting the listener in respect to person, place, time, and behavioural situation); the complicating action (the main body of narrative clauses which usually consists of a series of events); the resolution (the result of these events); the coda (a device for returning the verbal perspective to the present moment); and the evaluation (the point of the story).

A narrative as social practice approach reverses this tendency and considers the process of storytelling within the here and now context of its telling as a recipient-designed, fragmented, co-constructed, and emergent text that is necessarily designed to "do" something. In short, in De Fina and Georgakopoulou's (2008a: 381) terms, narratives are "enmeshed in local business, not free-standing or detached/detachable". Consequently, the focus of researchers taking a narrative as social practice approach extends to the "gamut of under-represented narrative activities, such as tellings of ongoing events, future or hypothetical events, and shared (known) events, but also allusions to (previous) tellings, deferrals of tellings, retellings, and refusals to tell" (De Fina & Johnstone, 2015: 157).

Taking such an approach to storytelling, rather than considering stories to be completed texts, favours an analytical focus on the emergent process of storytelling, its interactional details, and its embeddedness within a social process. This favours the use of transcripts of naturally occurring storytelling which are analysed using methods such as interactional sociolinguistics, which, grossly put, we define as an approach to analysis which, by closely observing a "speech event" in a particular community, focuses on language use in its social context. Interactional sociolinguistics traces its roots back to the pioneering work of Gumperz (1982). Gumperz (1982) drew on the insights of anthropology, linguistics, interactional pragmatics, and conversation analysis to provide an interpretive framework for analysing the way in which speakers signal and interpret meaning in social interaction. Moreover, interactional sociolinguistics is particularly interested in the way in which identity is negotiated in talk

(Bucholtz & Hall, 2005). Consequently, in this chapter, we pay particular attention to the way in which organisational identities (especially the identities of "them and us") are constructed in and through the social practice of storytelling.

Further, if you take an interactional sociolinguistic approach, you should base your analyses not only on the micro-level of interaction but also on extra-textual ethnographic knowledge that you have available (De Fina, 2021). In our case, for instance, we were already familiar with the team members, their work history, and their place in the hierarchy (Chapters 1 and 2). Furthermore, in Chapter 3, we have already seen the deep frictions caused by a major organisational restructuring, which provides the broad context for the interpretations of stories that are to follow. Orientation to such extra-textual context thus enables you to access the "taken-for-granted background assumptions that underlie the negotiation of shared interpretations" (Gumperz, 1999: 454) and which, therefore, inform the ways in which people do things such as storytelling (i.e. what gets told to whom, how, and when). Observations concerning the discursive strategies that the participants use to tell stories can then be juxtaposed with your knowledge of the extra-textual historical and social context in which the interaction occurred. Thus through being able to combine micro-analyses of talk (storytelling) with extra-textual ethnographic knowledge, interactional sociolinguistics as a research methodology enables you to capture the complexities of storytelling as a way of retrospectively making sense of the organisation. In this way, you can go beyond the micro-analyses of talk and scale up to issues of macro concern, or as De Fina and Georgakopoulou (2008a: 382) put it, a narrative as social practice approach: "attempts to synthesise the local occasioning of narratives in conversations with their role in a variety of macro-processes, such as the sanction of modes of knowledge accumulation and transmission, the exclusion and inclusion of social groups, the enactment of institutional routines, the perpetration of social roles, etc.". More specifically, therefore, taking a social practice approach to narratives, the purpose of this chapter is to provide a fine-grained analysis of rumours, as "unofficial" stories that attempt to make sense of what might be happening in the organisation, as they occur as part of mundane workplace practice. Moreover, in contrast to prior research into sense-making practices and storytelling, this chapter reveals what happens when sense is not made of the situation and the organisational story fails to provide coherence. We also illustrate that when sense of what is going on cannot be made, organisational players are obliged to take action that is less than optimal.

In what follows we showcase how you could use the lens of interactional linguistics to take a narrative as social practice approach to the analysis of storytelling as organisational practice. First and foremost, it is important to use naturally occurring interaction, i.e. that which is not elicited by the researcher in an interview. Or if interview talk is used, it should be analysed as interaction, paying attention to the situated nature of the talk using transcripts including both the interviewer's and the interviewee's turns at talk. See Darics and Clifton (2019) for an example of research that takes a narrative as social practice approach to stories told in interview situations. Once the transcription is complete and narratives have been isolated, then the researcher should begin to analyse the stories, intertwining their ethnographic knowledge of the organisation with an analysis of linguistic features, such as pronoun use, lexical choice, identity, or whatever so as to provide a fine-grained analysis of the way in which the participants make sense of the world around them. In the analysis, below we are particularly interested in the way in which the participants jointly construct the organisation in terms of a "them-and-us" dichotomy. Of course, elements of the storytelling can be analysed using vocabulary and concepts from structural analysis. However, the structure of the story per se is not what interests us; rather, we are interested in the storytelling as a social practice and a way of constructing meaning, in this case especially through the use of an "us-and-them" dichotomy. Key considerations guiding analysis would be the following. What pronouns are used and by whom? What actions are achieved through such pronominal use? What identities are made relevant for the speaker, audience, or non-present third parties by such pronominal use? What organisational identity is enacted through such pronominal use? How does the use of the "them-and-us" dichotomy make sense of the organisational world, and the social actors within it, and give it meaning? Further, because of our consultancy work, we were aware that the organisation was going through unpopular changes, and we guessed correctly that storytelling would be an area in which these differences would come out.

Data

In Chapter 1, we discussed in detail the broader context in which the income generation team operates. For the segments we zoom in on here, it is useful to remind ourselves that the team is relatively young. Amy was only hired 11 weeks prior to this discussion, and Kira had only been with the company for nine months. Judith had been working as a volunteer. As data for this chapter, we use transcripts of talk taken from a meeting between Kira, Amy, and Judith. The particular episode of storytelling talk analysed in this chapter comes just after the episode discussed in Chapter 4 in which Amy, Kira, and Judith discuss ways of raising awareness of the hospice and whose profile should appear in the local press—the leaders or the nurses. The analyses presented in this chapter focus on the way in which Amy, Kira, and Judith attempt to make sense of why the leaders appear to be reticent to have their profiles in the press and why they do not, or cannot, lead. They do this by presenting several plot lines that may explain what they perceive to be a failure in leadership and so make sense of the situation. Any one of these speculative stories (i.e. rumours) could become the story that makes sense of the organisational environment. However, findings indicate that none of the proposed stories make sense and so Amy, Kira, and Judith remain in a state of incomprehension: what has happened and is and will be happening in the organisation remains a chaotic flux of impressions which provides no direction for action.

Extract 5.1: The Story

In the prior talk Amy, Kira, and Judith have been discussing ways of persuading the leadership team to put their profiles in the newspaper (see Chapter 4). We join the talk as Amy evaluates the leadership team's lack of enthusiasm to have their profiles publicised and put in the press. This provides the necessary background with which to understand what is going on in the forthcoming storytelling.

Extract 5.1

1.	Amy	interesting isn't it I haven't come across that level of er:
2.		if it starts here where do you go
3.	Kira	they haven't had their review yet have they (.) or is going
4.		through it now
5.	Amy	what review↓
6.	Kira	you know [the resources had their review and restructure

7.	Amy	[appraisal
8.	Kira	it's the first directorship of the hospice to have gone through
9.		I remember Laura saying that she was going through that [on a
10.	Amy	[uhu
11.		more of er: down down-low
12.	Amy	oh really↓
13.	Kira	so they were getting ready to make changes for people
14.		are going and jobs are changing so probably right in the middle of
15.		what's = you know
16.		(.6)
17.	Amy	[you mean they might be nervous you mean
18.	Kira	[part part of it is °that°
19.	Amy	I don't think Paul would be nervous he can't be
20.		Pete's just started so he can't be he just has a
21.		problem with [being on the front line
22.	Kira	[nah no not about Paul it's just that
23.		they're trying to = they're saying there's an us and them
24.		thing when they're being instructed to to = there are
25.		changes being made but that's where the feeling is
26.		coming from but I don't think this [is going to °make°

In line 1, Amy offers a criticism of the leadership team, who don't want to lead (cf. Chapter 4). In line 3, Kira makes a topic transition from explicitly addressing why the leadership team don't want their profiles in the press to the reviews (i.e. business audits). Amy, line 5, displays that she has no knowledge of this review, and so Kira informs her that "the (human) resources have had their review and restructure" (lines 6–8) and that it is the first directorship of the hospice to have been through the process. The review and restructure refers to the process whereby all the employees were interviewed and their jobs were graded in terms of tier utility (see Chapter 1). A poor grading could result in being "let go". Thus, in the absence of knowledge of what is going on, they begin to speculate (rumour-monger) as to what is going on and why. Kira then begins a story in which she remembers Laura telling her that "she was going through that [i.e. a review and restructure] on a bit of a down down-low"[2] (line 11). Specific reference to the secrecy of the information, therefore, sets up the forthcoming story as something that is unofficial, unannounced, and unknown to outsiders and thus the very stuff of rumour. Amy receives this as news (line 12: "oh really"). Kira continues

[2] A down-low is a colloquial term that means in secret or discreetly.

the story informing Amy of the consequences of the review and restructure which are that "they were getting ready to make changes for people to go and jobs are changing". The upshot of this is not given; it is merely projected and given with reference to common knowledge: "so probably in the middle of what's = you know".

After this, there is a slight pause, and then Amy and Kira both self-select to take the next turn at the same time. Kira cedes the floor to Amy who formulates her understating of Kira's prior uncompleted turn: "you mean they might be nervous you mean" (line 17). In line 19 and following, Amy disagrees with Kira's (projected) formulation that they might be nervous and gives her assessment of the story, which is that she doesn't think Paul would be nervous, and Pete can't be nervous because he's just started but he does have a problem being in the front line. Kira aligns with this (line 22: "no not about Paul") and then accounts for where the feeling of nervousness is coming from. This is because it's just that they (i.e. the directorship of the hospice, cf. line 8) are trying to do something (lines 22–23: "it's just that they're trying to"). The complement of the verb (i.e. what they are trying to do) is not given. The talk in progress is cut off, and Kira self-corrects from what "they're trying to do" to what "they're saying", which is that "there's an us and them thing" (lines 23–24). So, the story is now that the directorship are saying that there is an "us and them thing" because "they are being instructed to". Kira does not finish her utterance, so exactly what the directors are being instructed to do, and by whom, is left hanging and corrected to the fact that "changes are being made" and that this is where the nervous feeling is coming from. Thus, in sum, the story is that there are changes afoot and these changes have resulted in a "feeling" of nervousness (and implicitly an explanation of why the directorship do not want their profiles to appear in the press). Significantly, the organisation is talked into being in terms of an "us-and-them" dichotomy. As Coupland et al. (2005) argue, such "us-and-them" dichotomies in the workplace talk into being not only two separate groups within the organisation but often groups (such as management and workers) who have different and potentially antagonistic interests which may therefore weaken the organisation—a point we return to later in the chapter.

Extract 5.2: The Nervous Feeling

In the prior talk, Kira has made sense of what is going on in the organisation (the "nervous feeling") by attributing it to the change that is happening. As the talk continues, Amy assesses and evaluates this sense-making and unravels the "us-and-them" identity work that Kira has set up.

Extract 5.2

27.	Amy	[but then that's never
28.		going to go if as a leader you don't understand that
29.		the organisation has to restructure (.) and that it's going to
30.		be painful.hhh (.7) I'm lost at the leadership wh-what do
31.		you think think's going to happen because if you can't
32.		afford it or the job is not valid it will go ultimately (.) so
33.		there's always going to be a them and us because can they fire
34.		you the answer is yes they can
35.	Kira	yeah and there's always this
36.	Amy	so it's it's a game = a game going on
37.	Kira	someone's the boss and someone's' not [there's always going to be
38.	Amy	[yeah
39.	Kira	an element of that [you can't get away from that you have to embrace =
40.	Amy	[yeah
41.		that's just part of being a manager [and not being a manager
42.	Amy	[yeah
43.	Kira	this culture of this them and us [=and last week there wasn't I-I
44.	Amy	[yeah
45.	Kira	just find it (.5) I find it all a bit bizarre

In line 26, Kira projects an evaluation of the identity work that has been done (i.e. the us-and-them situation), which is responsible for the (nervous) feeling: "but I don't think this is going to °make°". However, as her turn is in progress, she is overlapped by Amy who provides a possible evaluation to this identity work. She evaluates this specifically in terms of leadership and the failure of the leadership to "understand that the organisation has to restructure (.) and that it's going to be painful" (lines 28–30). The leaders of the hospice are thus talked into being inadequate (cf. Chapter 4) because they don't understand that restructuring leads to a painful feeling. This evaluation leaves Amy at a loss (line 30: "I'm lost"). Furthermore, the only way of making sense of the situation is to attribute it to a lack of leadership in which the leaders don't recognise that "if you can't afford it or the job is not valid it will go ultimately". Thus, Amy displays her understanding of the changes mentioned in the previous stories as those in which jobs will be cut, which, as Bordia et al. (2004) argue, is one of the key situations of change in which rumours become rife. The identity work that Amy does also explains the "us-and-them" situation to which Kira has alluded. "Them" are now clearly the management who can fire you (the others). The organisational world is now made sense of in a very dichotomous way: because of the changes occurring, those who can fire (the leaders) are set up in opposition to those who can be fired (the other employees), and this is leading to a painful feeling (line 30). In line 36, Amy sums up what is going on, evaluating it as a game ("so it's it's a game = a game going on").

Kira affiliates with this evaluation by elaborating the nature of the game and of the dichotomous organisational world. In this world, "someone's the boss and someone's not" and because of that "there's always going to be an element of that" (i.e. that the boss can sack the others in times of change). Kira's evaluation of this situation is that "you can't get away from that you have to embrace = that's just part of being a manager and not being a manager". This is again an implicit moral judgement of the management/leadership team not fulfilling their responsibilities. Thus, in this case at least, rumour is used to negatively evaluate the management.

Kira then evaluates this identity in terms of "this culture of them and us" and makes sense of what is happening in the workplace in terms of an "us-and-them" dichotomy which Kira claims wasn't there last week (line 43) and which she then evaluates as being "a bit bizarre" (line 45). In other words, she, and Amy through back-channelling agreement (line 44: yeah), makes sense of the organisational landscape only in terms of its bizarreness. Ironically, then, the sense of the situation is that there is no sense. In other words, the problem of deciding what the story is and so of retrospectively making sense of what is happening in the organisation by storying it has still not been resolved, or if it has been resolved, it is in negative terms by evaluating it as bizarre. However, the sense-making does not stop there, and in the following extract, Amy continues to speculate as to what is going on and why and offers several potential stories that could make sense of the bizarreness.

Extract 5.3: Three Possible Storylines Making Sense of the Nervous Feeling

In the continuing talk, Amy first tells Kira to "sit on it", i.e. not to spread rumours about the change and the "us-and-them" dichotomy that makes sense of the nervous feeling in terms of the dichotomy of the sackers and the sackable. After this advice, Amy continues to search for a story that makes sense of the situation.

Extract 5.3

46.	Amy	maybe maybe Kira sit on it maybe there is something happening
47.		at the Laura level in her department with Jo that's actually =
48.	Kira	= and that's making them nervous
49.	Amy	I dunno but it means that perhaps I just need to go = coz
50.		Pete's quite frank isn't he just need to go and sit and say
51.		what I need to understand is where this is coming from coz
52.		if it's coming because of that then I dunno quite what we do
53.		it's coming because you believe this and I'm not sure
54.		here is my reasoning for it and if it's coming because
55.		actually because truly you want to put your
56.		lovely team into you know it's because they're so brilliant
57.		and they wanna tell a story we need to have a plan to do
58.		that which is just you be default is not gonna work either
59.	?	euhum
60.	Amy	but what-what is the actual issue or is it because of all the bad
61.		press before that the some don't want to be head above the parapet

In line 46 and following, Amy seeks to make sense of the apparent bizarreness of the "us-and-them" story by speculating (signalled by the "maybe") that "maybe there is something happening at the Laura level in her department with Jo that's actually". This hypothetical story, therefore, attempts to make sense of the bizarreness of the situation, and so provides an explanation for the "us-and-them" dichotomy by speculating that there is something else going on, of which they have no knowledge. Lack of knowledge and lack of an official story thus become a motor for speculative sense-making and the rumour-mongering that is going on. Kira, line 48, then adds an increment, signalled by the "and", to Amy's turn in progress (line 48: "and that's making them nervous"). This provides a coda to the story (i.e. the nervousness is attributed to the changes) which explains why they (the management/leadership team) are nervous. It also returns to the possible story (as discussed in Extract 5.1) in which the management team are nervous because of the changes going on.

Citing her lack of knowledge (line 49: "I dunno"), Amy doesn't align with the storyline. In order to resolve the issue, she speculates that she just needs to go to see Pete "coz he's quite frank" and say: "what I need to understand is where this is coming from". The "this" is vague, but considering the immediately prior talk, it is reasonably heard as the "them-and-us" situation, the bad feeling, and ultimately the reason why the management team do not want their profiles to appear in the press (cf. Chapter 4, which discusses this point at length). In this future story in which Amy goes to see Pete, she will set out two alternatives. The first is that "it's coming because of that". The pronominal use makes the referent of this utterance vague, but considering the prior talk, it can be interpreted as the "us-and-them" situation that has been made relevant and "that" is the nervousness, stemming from the changes, that has led them to be shy of putting their profiles in the press. If this sense-making is correct and if this is the organisational story, then Amy doesn't know how to react (line 52: "I dunno quite what we do"). The inability to make sense and the lack of an official story which makes sense, therefore, have negative effects on the organisation: How can one act in the organisational landscape if one cannot make sense of it? In classic leadership terms, the leadership has been unsuccessful because it has failed to set a direction, develop vision, and provide a coherent story that not only accounts for change but also is communicated in such a way as to persuade the organisational players to commit to this vision and to work towards it (Nanus, 1992).

The second story which would explain the "us-and-them" dichotomy is that the management/leadership team want to put their "lovely team" into the press (lines 54 ff.). This story returns to the question of whose profile should go in the newspaper (cf. Chapter 4) and makes sense of the leaders' reluctance to have their profile in the press because they want to tell their story and so implicitly do not want to pass via Amy and Kira. This storyline is laced with sarcasm, as indicated by the exaggerated adjectives the "lovely team" who are so "brilliant". However, if this is the case, Amy argues that they need a plan and the management team being default is not going to work (line 58). This plot line thus does identity work that sustains the "us-and-them" dichotomy in the organisation, while attributing a deviant identity to the management who have no plan. Again, such an unofficial story is not flattering to the management who are talked into not only having different interests to those of the fundraising team but they are also storied as acting on these interests behind the backs of Kate and Amy.

However, the "actual issue" (i.e. the underlying story that makes sense of the situation) still escapes Amy who projects a third possible story which makes sense of the situation. The third alternative is that "because of all the bad press before that the some don't want to be head above the parapet". This explains the management team's reticence to have their profile in the press on account of the bad press they had before. This was especially related to a recent incident in which a key fundraiser, who had become somewhat of a local celebrity, was forced out by the new management changes. On account of her popularity, the management team had received a lot of adverse publicity for letting her go.

Extract 5.4: "So Fuck It" and the Consequences of a Failure in Sense-making

After these three possible storylines are mentioned, there is a slight pause before Kira begins a turn with "so" which projects the coda, or the upshot, of these stories and their relevance in the here and now.

Extract 5.4

62.	?	erm
63.		(.7)
64.	Kira	so
65.	Amy	so fuck it
66.	Kira	((slight laugh)) did you say fuck it or bucket
67.	Amy	I dunno I think I said fuck [it
68.	?	[((slight laugh))
69.	Amy	erm I think we need to have a patient story just in case

Despite Kate's projection of a coda, signally by "so" (line 64), it is Amy who completes it: "fuck it". As Jay and Janschewitz (2008: 267) point out, one of the functions of swearing is to express emotions, especially anger and frustration, and so in this case Amy's utterance is hearable as anger and frustration at the fact that she cannot make sense of the situation (i.e. why doesn't the management team want to put their profile in the press). In short, considering the lack of an official story, she and Kira resort to rumour (i.e. hypothetical stories of what might be happening). However, these rumours still do not make sense out of what is going on and this leads to anger and frustration which reinforces an antagonistic "us-and-them" way of perceiving the organisation. The "them" is composed of the directorship who are talked into being nervous on account of the forthcoming changes and are failing in their leadership. The "us" are the sackable (cf. line 32), which includes Kate and Amy and the fundraising team. Further, not making sense paves the way for a plan

B, which is to have a patient's story to go in the press "just in case" (line 69), and thus indicates that a lack of sense sets up a course of action that is acceptable but not desired, i.e. a plan B rather than a plan A.

Observations

This chapter set out to provide a fine-grained analysis of rumours that are designed by organisational players to make sense of the organisational world and act upon it. First, we note that, in the absence of an official story that makes sense of what is going on, several hypothetical and unofficial stories—rumours—emerge that attempt to make sense of the organisation. Second, we argue that if none of these unofficial stories make sense of the organisation, then storytellers/organisational players are unable to act or are forced to act in ways that are less than optimal for the organisation. Third, we conclude that, regardless of whether sense is made of the organisation or not, the hypothetical stories of what might be going on nevertheless define the organisation in a particular way—in this case, there is an antagonistic "us-and-them" dichotomy.

In the absence of an official story, rumour/unofficial stories emerge as a way of making sense of what is happening. Specifically, in Extract 5.1, we observe that sense is made of this situation through the unofficial story that the leadership team are undergoing a review and restructure in which people might "go". Further, in Extract 5.3, Amy offers three different hypothetical stories that attempt to make sense of the fact that the leadership team do not want to put their profiles in the press, namely: the review and restructure is making them nervous; the leadership team want to put their own profiles in the paper, implicitly not passing through Amy; and because of bad press they do not want to "put their heads above the parapet".

It is noticeable that these unofficial stories are speculative and driven by a lack of knowledge of what is going on, which is seen throughout the storytelling. Thus, concurring with prior research on rumours, it is clear that a state of unknowing leads to speculative stories. Also, since these stories are based on a lack of knowledge, it is not surprising that none of the storytellers are able to make sense of the organisational landscape. And, despite setting out at least three different stories that could possibly make sense of the organisation, none of the stories is chosen as *the* story that makes sense. Consequently, the situation remains *senseless* and this leads Amy to express dissatisfaction with the situation ("oh fuck it") and to set out a plan B, i.e. to have a patient story ready just in case. The inability to make sense of the organisation through providing a plausible narrative thus, to some extent, paralyses the organisational players and in frustration they prepare for a course of action that is non-optimal (i.e. a plan B).

Further, regardless of whether one story emerges that makes sense of what is happening or not, and regardless of whether the organisational players are able to act on this sense-making or not, the process of attempting to make sense of events through unofficial storytelling of what might be the case talks the organisation into being as a divided and fractured one. On the one side, there is the "them", which is the leadership team, and on the other side, there is the "us", who are the employees. The leadership team do the firing and the employees are subject to being fired, and it is this that is potentially causing a nervous feeling (Extract 5.2). The organisation is thus talked into being as split, and it is this divide that is having negative effects on the organisation and causing nervousness. Moreover, this dichotomous understanding of the organisation becomes a moral issue. Notably, in Extract 5.3, Amy criticises the leadership team for not understanding that the organisation has to restructure and that jobs might go. Thus, the "them" (i.e. the leadership team) is talked into being as in some way deviant and not capable of doing their job (cf. Chapter 4—"the leadership team don't want to lead").

Further, it is significant that these stories emerge on account of the lack of an official organisational story. First, it is noticeable that the attempts to find a story that makes sense of the organisation are triggered by the uncertainty generated by the secretive way in which the review and restructure was carried out. Thus, we argue that doing something secretly, especially when it may result in job losses, is inadvisable since it could lead to a search for an unofficial story that makes sense of the situation in a way that the leadership does not intend. Moreover, such an unofficial story, as in the stories analysed in this chapter which enact both a failing leadership team and a divided organisation (them and us), may well be negative. Therefore, the findings of this chapter concur with work on leadership/organisational storytelling that argues that the role of leaders/managers is to provide and disseminate "good" stories which account for what was/is/will be happening in the organisation (Fleming, 2001). In other words, in times of change the leadership of the organisation should ensure that the official story is clear and transparent. Without such an official story that makes sense of the changes, numerous unofficial stories may circulate and these may not present the changes in a flattering light. However, not being open about what is going on in a company and not providing an official story is not only the preserve of the leadership. After all, Amy also advises Kira to "sit on it" and not reveal what she knows (Extract 5.3). Thus, through not providing official stories, it is possible that a climate of distrust and secrecy is installed and that this becomes pervasive in the organisation.

Thus far, there is nothing in these findings that would raise the eyebrows of organisational scholars who would widely agree that rumour thrives when official stories are absent, which may lead to a lack of trust within the organisation and may portray the protagonists of the story, in this case the leadership team, in a bad light. However, we argue that while the findings of this chapter concur with research on rumour, we also note that what is lacking in previous research is a fine-grained analysis of how rumours actually occur. For example, Boje (1995: 1001), in his seminal paper on storytelling, notes that "organisations cannot be registered as one story, but instead are a multiplicity, a plurality of stories and story interpretations in struggle with one another". However, while noting this, he did not seek to provide a fine-grained analysis of stories in the making. Conversely, taking a narrative as social practice approach to unofficial narratives/rumours in the making enables us to make visible the ways in which a multiplicity of speculative narratives emerge as part of naturally occurring workplace activity in an attempt to make sense of what is going on. An interactional sociolinguistic approach to rumour thus provides empirical evidence of the plurivocality of storytelling and how speculative unofficial stories emerge, and of the possibly toxic effects that such rumours may engender such as talking the organisation into being as one which is divided and constituted by an antagonistic "us-and-them" dichotomy.

Conclusions

Many organisational scholars, notably Weick (1995), have argued that stories are prime sites for meaning-making. However, few of them have used a narrative approach to organisation to demonstrate the in situ practice of storytelling through which sense-making is achieved. In this chapter, we have given a narrative as social practice twist to work on rumour, which to date has been dominated by work based on interviews or surveys. Interview- and survey-based research gives researchers access to what organisational players *say* rumour is and to what they retrospectively *say* they think rumour does, but it does not give the researcher access to the "doing" of rumour as an in situ accomplishment. Conversely, taking a narrative as social practice approach to rumour demonstrates how rumour emerges as part of mundane workplace activity. To some extent, these findings concur with, and confirm, existing work on rumour that claims that it is driven by a lack of knowledge and of top-down (official) communication, and that it can lead to the emergence of alternative and potentially damaging narratives. However, studying rumour as it emerges is important because it shifts the focus of research away from how leaders are managers of meaning (Smircich & Morgan, 1982) to reveal the way in which other employees are also engaged in authoring new realities that may provide counternarratives and which construct the organisational landscape in "unofficial" ways.

In this case rumour talks the organisation into being as a dichotomous one with an "us-and-them" rift between senior management and employees which has negative effects on the organisation. We know from our consultancy work that the organisation was deeply divided on account of the restructuring, new methods of working that were being introduced, and the "letting go" of some staff members, including the previous fundraising manager. This in situ identity work is important because it is not "just" a reflection of the organisation; rather, it constructs, or stories into being, the organisational landscape in a particular way. Moreover, once talked into being in a particular way, the organisational landscape is oriented to as a structure that constrains and allows action and ways of being. Consequently, from a social constructionist perspective, the nervousness and the antagonist split between employees and leaders become more than a story/rumour. They become a conversational reality (Shotter, 1993) upon which organisational players base their actions and, in this case, since the participants cannot make sense of the organisation, there is a paralysis of action—or at least a choice of action that is less than optimal for the organisation. Therefore, adopting a social practice approach to narrative could provide you with a lens for the investigation of workplace activities that shows the processes through which storytelling is achieved and how these impact on the organisation and wider (macro) organisational concerns such as change management, organisational identity, and so on.

References

Allport, G., & Postman, L. (1947). *The psychology of rumor*. Holt, Rinehart and Winston.

Balogun, J. (2007). The practice of organizational restructuring: From design to reality. *European Management Journal, 25*(2), 81–91.

Boje, D. (1995). Stories of the storytelling organization: A postmodern analysis of Disney as "Tamara-Land." *Academy of Management Journal, 38*(4), 997–1035.

Boje, D. (2001). *Narrative methods for organizational and communication research*. Sage.

Boje, D. (2008). *Storytelling organizations*. Sage.

Bondielli, A., & Marcelloni, F. (2019). A survey on fake news and rumour detection techniques. *Information Sciences, 497*, 38–55.

Bordia, P., Hobman, E., Jones, E., Gallois, C., & Callan, V. J. (2004). Uncertainty during organizational change: Types, consequences, and management strategies. *Journal of Business and Psychology, 18*(4), 507–532.

Bordia, P., Jones, E., Gallois, C., Callan, V. J., & DiFonzo, N. (2006). Management are aliens! Rumors and stress during organizational change. *Group & Organization Management, 31*(5), 601–621.

Bucholtz, M., & Hall, K. (2005). Identity and interaction: A sociocultural linguistic approach. *Discourse Studies, 7*(4–5), 585–614.

Chia, R. (2000). Discourse analysis as organizational analysis. *Organisation, 7*(3), 513–518.

Coupland, C., Blyton, P., & Bacon, N. (2005). A longitudinal study of the influence of shop floor work teams on expressions of 'us' and 'them.' *Human Relations, 58*(8), 1055–1081.

Darics, E., & Clifton, J. (2019). Making applied linguistics applicable to business practice: Discourse analysis as a management tool. *Applied Linguistics, 40*(6), 917–936.

De Fina, A. (2021). Doing narrative analysis from a narratives-as-practices perspective. *Narrative Inquiry, 31*(1), 49–71.

De Fina, A., & Georgakopoulou, A. (2008a). Analysing narratives as practices. *Qualitative Research, 8*(3), 379–387.

De Fina, A., & Georgakopoulou, A. (2008b). Introduction: Narrative analysis in the shift from texts to practices. *Text & Talk, 28*(3), 275–281.

De Fina, A., & Georgakopoulou, A. (2015). Introduction. In A. De Fina & A. Georgakopoulou (Eds.), *The handbook of narrative analysis* (pp. 1–17). Wiley Blackwell.

De Fina, A., & Johnstone, B. (2015). Discourse analysis and narrative. In D. Tannen, H. Hamilton, & D. Schiffrin (Eds.), *The handbook of discourse analysis* (2nd ed., pp. 152–167). Wiley.

DiFonzo, N., & Bordia, P. (1998). A tale of two corporations: Managing uncertainty during organizational change. *Human Resource Management, 37*(3–4), 295–303.

Fenton, C., & Langley, A. (2011). Strategy as practice and the narrative turn. *Organization Studies, 32*(9), 1171–1196.

Fleming, D. (2001). Narrative leadership: Using the power of stories. *Strategy & Leadership, 29*(4), 34–36.

Georgakopoulou, A. (2011). Narrative. In J. Zienkowski, J. Ostam, & J. Verschueren (Eds.), *Discursive pragmatics* (pp. 190–207). John Benjamins.

Gumperz, J. (1982). *Discourse strategies*. Cambridge University Press.

Gumperz, J. (1999). On interactional sociolinguistic method. In C. Roberts & S. Sarangi (Eds.), *Talk, work and institutional order: Discourse in medical, mediation and management settings* (pp. 453–473). Mouton De Gruyter.

Jay, T., & Janschewitz, K. (2008). The pragmatics of swearing. *Journal of Politeness Research, 4*(2), 267–288.

Labov, W., & Waletzky, J. (1967). Narrative analysis: Oral versions of personal experience. In J. Helm (Ed.), *Essays on the verbal and visual arts*. University of Washington Press

Liff, R., & Wikström, E. (2021). Rumours and gossip demand continuous action by managers in daily working life. *Culture and Organization, 27*(6), 456–475.

Michelson, G., & Mouly, V. S. (2000). Rumour and gossip in organisations: A conceptual study. *Management Decision, 38*(5), 339–346.

Michelson, G., & Mouly, V. S. (2002). 'You didn't hear it from us but...': Towards an understanding of rumour and gossip in organisations. *Australian Journal of Management*, *27*(1_suppl), 57–65.

Michelson, G., & Mouly, V. S. (2004). Do loose lips sink ships? *Corporate Communications: An International Journal, 9*(3), 189–201.

Nanus, B. (1992). *Visionary leadership: Creating a compelling sense of direction for your organization*. Jossey-Bass.

Rhodes, C., & Brown, A. D. (2005). Narrative, organizations and research. *International Journal of Management Reviews, 7*(3), 167–188.

Rosnow, R. L. (1991). Inside rumor: A personal journey. *American Psychologist, 46*(5), 484–496.

Shotter, J (1993). *Conversational realities: Constructing life through language*. Sage.

Smircich, L., & Morgan, G. (1982). Leadership: The management of meaning. *The Journal of Applied Behavioral Science, 18*(3), 257–273.

Spear, S., & Roper, S. (2016). Storytelling in organisations: Supporting or subverting corporate strategy? *Corporate Communications: An International Journal, 21*(4), 516–532.

Vaara, E., Sonenshein, S., & Boje, D. (2016). Narratives as sources of stability and change in organizations: Approaches and directions for future research. *The Academy of Management Annals, 10*(1), 495–560.

Van De Mieroop, D., Clifton, J., & Schnurr, S. (2022). Narratives as social practice in organisational contexts. *Narrative Inquiry, 32*(1), 1–8.

Waddington, K. (2021). *Gossip, organization and work: A research overview*. Routledge.

Weick, K. E. (1995). *Sense-making in organizations*. Sage.

Weick, K. E. (2012). Organized sense-making: A commentary on processes of interpretive work. *Human Relations, 65*(1), 141–153.

CHAPTER 6

Tracking the Identity of the Organisation via Twitter: Metadiscourse Analysis

Introduction

Organisational identity has long been recognised as a key element in shaping how an organisation is perceived both internally and externally. It comprises organisational members' core values, beliefs, and principles and their perceptions about who they are as an organisation (Ravasi & Van Rekom, 2003; Whetten, 2006). Organisational identity is a key construct that guides the organisation's strategic decisions (Kjærgaard, 2009) and interactions with various stakeholders, both internal (Madsen, 2016) and external (Sillince & Brown, 2009). Over the past few decades, researchers have predominantly focused on analysing internal communication within organisations to understand the formation and evolution of organisational identity (for a review, see Brown, 2015; He & Brown, 2013). While this view provides valuable insights into the identity-building process, it often overlooks the role of external communication in crafting and maintaining an organisation's identity. In today's highly connected world, social media platforms have become essential tools for organisations to engage with their audiences, convey their messages, and shape both their public image and internal organisational identities (Di Lauro et al., 2020). As Cheney and Christensen (2001) argue, it is now crucial to examine evidence of organisational identity beyond the walls of the office and explore external

E. Darics and J. Clifton, *Organisation, Communication and Language*, New Perspectives in Organizational Communication,
https://doi.org/10.1007/978-3-031-30199-5_6

communication artefacts to gain a comprehensive understanding of how an organisation's identity is communicated and perceived by its audience.

This chapter aims to fill this gap in the literature by combining insights from organisational identity research with metadiscourse analysis, a discourse-analytical approach traditionally used to explore written texts. We argue that close, language-focused analysis of external communication, such as social media content, is essential for obtaining a more holistic understanding of the problems and challenges associated with organisational identity, particularly in situations where internal fragmentation transpires into external corporate communication. By focusing on elements of language that enable written texts to be dialogic and interpersonal—i.e. metadiscourse—we can expose potential problems that arise when misaligned organisational identity inadvertently projects discrepancies in external communications.

Due to such potential issues arising from the lack of a consistent and unified organisational identity, it is unsurprising that identity is a crucial element of organisational change processes (Mills et al., 2005), as we see in our case study of this team. During a change process, previous organisational structures and practices are in flux, and organisational members rely more heavily—if not exclusively—on their shared beliefs, conceptualisations about the organisation, and its goals. During such times, as Albert et al. (2000: 13) note, "a sense of identity serves as a rudder for navigating difficult waters", and for that reason "it becomes more important to have an internalised cognitive structure of what the organisation stands for and where it intends to go – in short, a clear sense of the organisation's identity".

Turning to the organisation of our case study, in the previous chapters we saw how organisational members were struggling to make sense of management decisions and their rapidly changing organisational reality. This negatively affected—or perhaps even paralysed—the team's efficiency: in fact, this was the very reason why the team leader commissioned our consultancy. The radically different conceptualisations (Chapter 3), the us-and-them dichotomy (Chapter 4), and the criticism articulated about the upper management's leadership (Chapter 5) revealed that the team members' perceptions of their own group, organisational leadership, common goals, and direction were incoherent. Their organisational identity was fragmented. This realisation provides a rationale for taking organisational identity as a conceptual starting point for this chapter, but we make a case for approaching it from a perspective that has received little attention in organisational discourse research. We propose that the organisation's voice, or the way in which it communicates, plays a significant role in constructing and maintaining a coherent and credible image. In this chapter, we will show that if we examine not just the content but also the manner in which messages are conveyed, we can reveal potential discrepancies between the internal and external manifestations of an organisation's identity. Focusing on social media communication, specifically Twitter, the chapter makes a case for using linguistic analysis to expose the complex relationship between internal and external organisational identity.

The chapter is structured as follows. First, we review scholarship that explores organisational identity with a combined analytical focus on internal and external communication. We introduce metadiscourse analysis and demonstrate how it can be applied to social media data to uncover evidence related to (problems with) organisational identity. Finally, we reposition the findings of the analysis in the broader context of the fundraising team and the entire organisation to expose the effects of identity fragmentation, and highlight the need to address any fragmentation to ensure the organisation's success.

Conceptualisations of Organisational Identity

The extensive body of research on organisational identity covers a wide range of perspectives and approaches. Although a comprehensive review is beyond the scope of this chapter, we recommend consulting He and Brown (2013), Brown (2015), Ravasi and Van Rekom (2003), and Ravasi and Canato (2013) for a more in-depth exploration. Here, we will focus our discussion on the differing conceptual starting points of organisational identity, as these distinctions influence the research focus and methodology.

On one hand, organisational identity can be viewed as *static*—something an organisation possesses which can be identified, described, and potentially managed (e.g. Whetten, 2006). He and Brown (2013: 6) emphasise that this approach examines identity through objective and tangible features, and to locate these, researchers explore sources such as official organisational histories, speeches, documents, physical attributes, or logos. This perspective assumes a certain stability and uniformity in the organisation's identity. On the other hand, the *dynamic* or *process* view of identity highlights the ongoing negotiation and development of shared understanding among organisational members. This approach focuses on the active construction of identity, and to explore this process, researchers examine the activities of organisational members (e.g. Harrison, 2000), artefacts involved in the sense-making process (Mills et al., 2005), internal interactions (e.g. Madsen, 2016), or focus group discussions (Henderson et al., 2015). Rooted in social constructivism, this perspective aligns with the central premise of this book: the constitutive role of communication we have emphasised in each chapter thus far. Compared to static and stable attributes, dynamic processes do not lend themselves as easily to scientific exploration, and as Svenningson and Alvesson (2003: 1164) note, relatively few empirical studies actually address specific processes of identity construction, with exceptions such as Alvesson (1994), Coupland and Brown (2004), and Madsen (2016). However, this assertion may hold more weight in organisation studies, as discourse analytic-linguistic literature, particularly within sociolinguistics (Bucholtz & Hall, 2005), and workplace discourse offer numerous examples of empirical, language-focused approaches to the in situ discursive construction of identity. Readers may find notable examples in Angouri and Marra's (2011) edited volume *Constructing Identities at Work* and Van De Mieroop and Schnurr's (2017) volume *Identity Struggles: Evidence from Workplaces around the World*.

In this chapter, we remain within the social constructivist paradigm but zoom out to focus on organisational identity in relation to the broader context of the organisation—the external stakeholders. To achieve this, we adopt a broader perspective that examines the interconnectedness of internal and external organisational communication, rather than delving into the linguistic details of interpersonal interactions or interviews. Below, we explore literature focusing on the interplay between internal and external communication and propose a greater consideration of both areas for the exploration of organisational identities and how they affect organisational processes.

The Interconnectedness of Internal and External Communication

The interconnected nature of internal and external communication in shaping organisational identities can be aptly illustrated through the metaphor of a glass door. This metaphor enables us to view the boundary between the organisation and the outside world both as a (transparent) barrier and as a point of connection. In the first conceptualisation, the barrier aspect highlights the visibility the glass door provides in both directions. Looking in from the outside, the degree of transparency may vary, but the glass door still offers external stakeholders a glimpse into the inner workings of the organisation. However, the organisational identity these onlookers perceive may not present a coherent picture. Scholarship has demonstrated that organisational identity is often polyphonic (Harrison, 2000) with identities that can be vague and conflicting (Mills et al., 2005; Sillince & Brown, 2009) or distinct and co-existing (Henderson et al., 2015). Whatever the image, though, it will affect the onlooker, especially if the image they see does not correspond to the corporate identity the organisation wishes to project, corporate identity being the distinctive public image that the organisation consciously communicates (Cornelissen et al., 2007).

The transparent barrier of the glass door also allows organisational members to look out, enabling them to observe how outsiders view the organisation. This phenomenon is referred to as the "construed external image" (Dutton et al., 1994: 248), which captures organisational members' beliefs about how their organisation and its members' behaviour are likely to be perceived by external stakeholders. Prior research indicates that these perceptions can significantly impact the formation or development of organisational identities (Dutton et al., 1994), and, if the image is unfavourable, it can affect the psychological well-being of organisational members (Elsbach & Kramer, 1996).

In addition to its function as a transparent barrier that lets information pass through, the glass door metaphor also emphasises the door as a point of connection for communication. This perspective highlights the co-constructed nature of organisational identity and suggests that neither internal nor external communication exists as a one-way process. Instead, they form a continuous dialogue between organisations and their stakeholders. With regard to internal members, research has shown that an incoherent organisational identity can "leak" into externally facing communications. Unspoken assumptions and a problematic organisational culture from within the organisation may subtly find their way into other areas of communication (Koller & Ereaut, 2020: 93). Following this logic, organisational members with a misaligned or inconsistent organisational identity can inadvertently project these discrepancies in their external communications, which as a result will fail to convince, or in worst cases alienate, external audiences (Fombrun & Rindova, 2000).

This observation is particularly true for the organisational unit in our case study, which needs to achieve its core aim of motivating the public to contribute to fundraising activities or indeed to donate money through a range of external communicative activities. To succeed, these messages should communicate a coherent, credible image of the organisation, imparted in a unified voice from within (Rogala, 2016).

Turning back to the metaphor of the glass door as a point of connection, just as communications originating from within the organisation play key roles in the co-construction of organisational images for self- and externally projected identity, equally important are the interactions that originate from the outside. As Cheney and Christensen (2001) note, these dialogues have become increasingly important for the way in which organisations manage the perceptions of the public, (re)gain trust, and consequently legitimise their corporate brand. Coupland and Brown (2004), for example, explore this collaborative identity work through the analysis of two email exchanges that were posted on Royal Dutch/Shell's website. Through the close discourse-analytic examination of the exchange between outsiders and organisational representatives, Coupland and Brown tracked the discursive co-construction of the organisation's identity and attest that "organizational identities, and cognates such as image and reputation, are not singular or unitary 'things' that can be simply observed and easily measured. Rather, they are emergent aspects of an organization-centred discourse" (Coupland & Brown, 2004: 1341).

A Case in Point: The Hospice

In the case of our local hospice, since it is so closely embedded in, and working with and for, the community, two-way perceptions and communication between the public and the organisation is crucially important (see also the conversation about community publication in Chapter 5). To illustrate this, let's examine the extract from Kira's interview, one of the youngest members of the team:

Extract 6.1

1.	Kira:	I think social media's important to err a lot of people a lot of people will pick
2.		things up on social media (.) when I first started looking back at what had been
3.		done before because I-I thought I'd better see how erm I think people had
4.		spoken before there were a lot of complaints about the restructure that just

5. weren't responded to an-and from what I learnt in uni you need to respond
6. otherwise it builds in people

In this extract, Kira talks about her role as a social media manager. She recalls taking over the social media manager task by focusing on the lack of response to the backlash about the organisational restructuring on social media. Kira's comment exposes two interrelated issues: first, the communication from the outside in, and second, the communication from the inside out. We will unpack these to illustrate why they are relevant for organisational identity. In the first case, external stakeholders took to social media to express their criticism of internal organisational change processes. This instance proves what Cheney and Christensen (2001) call the "fuzziness of organisational boundaries": we illustrated this phenomenon using the glass door metaphor above. New communication technologies, especially social media, have provided increased opportunities for the public to "talk back" (e.g. Coupland & Brown, 2004; Di Lauro et al., 2020), challenge and influence organisational processes (Jameson, 2014), and express explicit criticism, as we saw in Extract 6.1. Such messages, whether designed to provide feedback or influence action, send a very clear message about the public's perception of the organisation's identity, and as we explained above, this perception can in turn influence the (construction of) organisational identity (Dutton et al., 1994).

The criticism from external stakeholders, as our respondent notes above, was left unanswered. This comment leads us to the second issue, namely the communicative behaviour of the organisation itself. Organisations as a whole are engaged in interactions with external stakeholders through a variety of channels—from the logo greeting the visitors over the main entrance to emails and phone calls from individual employees to corporate communication channels such as the website and social media. Corporate communication channels are, of course, the primary channels where an organisation consciously aims to project its (preferred) public image, its corporate identity. These channels of communication are, mainly, controlled and managed, although as research shows, fragmented or multiple organisational identities are likely to manifest themselves through these channels, too. Based on the analysis of internal and external communication documents, interviews, and observations in a UK-based charity, Koller and Ereaut (2020: 97) exposed how the actual language used in promotional materials projected an educated but detached, impersonal, middle-class identity, causing a mismatch between projected and preferred organisational identities. Based on rhetorical analysis of police websites, Sillince and Brown (2009) found that even within the same communicative context, an organisation can project multiple identities. In the case of Kira's commentary (Extract 6.1), it is not so much what the organisation said or did that is revealing but rather the lack of action. It is now common knowledge that negative comments or criticism on social media can quickly spread and potentially harm an organisation's reputation, and these need to be addressed and responded to in a timely manner. Kira makes this knowledge relevant by referring to her university studies (line 5). Leaving criticism unattended may suggest an organisation's lack of concern for its public image, which may lead to negative perceptions that can reveal a disconnect between the organisation's internal values and external mission (Fombrun & Rindova, 2000; Rogala, 2016).

In the previous sections, we reviewed scholarship and used a specific example from our case study to illustrate the importance of the bi-directional (intentional and unintentional) communication between external stakeholders and internal organisational members as a means of constructing, negotiating, and confirming organisational identities. We repeatedly emphasised the significance of examining the process through which organisational identity is formed, as well as how it influences perception and action, both externally and internally. The literature review has also shown what the examination of external communication activities can reveal about the inner workings of an organisation, proving, as Cheney and Christensen (2001) argue, that "external communication activities of contemporary organisations must be seen as closely connected to those presumably inside the container of the organisation".

In this chapter, we will use data from social media—specifically Twitter—to further this line of study. Using close, language-focused discourse analysis, we will showcase what we can learn about organisational identity through linguistic strategies used by the members of the fundraising team.

Data and Methodology

The hospice at the time of our consultancy had both a Facebook and a Twitter account, but neither were used very actively. In the summer months, they only posted two posts on their Facebook account, both of which were photo albums with little text. Therefore, we focused our attention on their Twitter account. We were planning to collect their Twitter activity around the time of our visit in August, but due to the low number of tweets, we extended the observed period to six months: this period yielded 34 tweets. Their Twitter followership was at around 3,000 and direct engagement with the tweets (likes, shares, comments) was minimal. Their inactivity on social media was perhaps symptomatic of the problems that initiated the consultancy, and since then, activity on both accounts has increased considerably.

Irrespective of whether it was efficient or not, the organisation's social media channel was still worthy of examination because, as we have argued above, it provided an expression of the organisation's voice and consequently their organisational identity. The tweets were analysed in their entirety. However, for reasons of confidentiality, the actual tweets presented below are edited. Data, such as weblinks and self- and geographic references, that would make the tweets recognisable were deleted.

The voice of the "organisation-as-rhetor" (Sillince & Brown, 2009) has been explored in previous literature by looking at distinctive features in language use, for example, typical vocabulary and pragmatic features such as hedging (Koller & Ereaut, 2020), rhetorical devices (Sillince & Brown, 2009), or the close reading for salient features (Coupland & Brown, 2004). In this chapter, we apply an analytical approach referred to as metadiscourse analysis.

Metadiscourse Analysis

Metadiscourse refers to the language used by writers or speakers to create interaction between their texts and the readers/listeners (Hyland, 2005). It is language use which explicitly guides the reader or listener through the text, makes the structure and argument clear, and establishes a relationship with the audience. It is a way for writers to establish their authority and create a sense of community with their readers. Scholarship traditionally distinguishes between two types of metadiscourse: one is text-oriented, focusing on language which refers to the text itself, signalling its direction, purpose, and internal structure (Table 6.1), and the other is personal-oriented, which aims to capture language that helps to engage the reader and enables the writer to express their stance, attitude, and identity in relation to the content and the reader (Table 6.2). More recently, as digitally mediated communication has blurred the boundaries between speech and writing (Darics, 2015), scholars have drawn on metadiscourse to capture how interactivity is inscribed in digitally mediated text (see D'Angelo et al., 2021). This line of scholarship has directed attention to discourse features typical of digitally mediated texts, identifying a range of resources that serve as metadiscourse devices, such as hashtags, mentions, hypothetical answers, or simulated dialogue (Vásquez, 2015; Zappavigna, 2018). Several of these, as shown in Tables 6.1 and 6.2, do not fit neatly into the text-oriented and personal-oriented categories, and their function to create engagement between writer and reader lies precisely in the ambiguity of their role (see Love et al., 2023).

Table 6.1 Text-oriented metadiscourse (based on Hyland, 2005, 2017; Zappavigna, 2018)

Text-oriented metadiscourse	*Definition*	*Examples*
Transition markers	Convey the relations between main clauses	however, firstly, therefore, and
Frame markers	Refer to discourse acts, sequences, or stages	finally, to conclude, my purpose is
Endophoric markers	Refer to information in other parts of the text	see Fig. 1, noted above, as discussed below
Code glosses	Elaborate propositional meanings	namely, for example, such as, in other words
Evidentials	Refer to information from other texts	according to Smith (2010), Z states, as reported by X
Hashtags[1]	Indicate topics or keywords	#hospiceweek
Retweets	Indicate the reposting of another user's tweet	RT @LinguaDigitalis
Links	Indicate web addresses	http://bit.ly/2RZjwXXX

[1] Please note hashtags can function as interactional metadiscourse devices (see Zappavigna, 2018).

Table 6.2 Interactional metadiscourse (based on Biri, 2021; Hyland, 2005; Vásquez, 2015)

Interactional metadiscourse	*Definition*	*Examples*
Self-mentions	Explicit reference to author as discourse participant	I, me, my, our, mine, us, we
Audience mention	Explicitly address or involve readers in the text	you, your, let us, consider
Collective mention	Includes the reference to writer and reader as collective participants[2]	we, our, let's
Hedges	Withhold full commitment to propositions and recognise alternative voices and viewpoints	might, perhaps, possible, tend
Boosters	Express certainty and emphasise propositions and the writer's confidence in them	clearly, definitely, obviously, in fact
Attitude markers	Express the writer's affective attitude to propositions	unfortunately, surprisingly, fortunately
Discourse markers	Marking writing as "speech-like"	well, you know, oh
Questions	Use interrogatives to directly address or involve readers in the text	Do you agree? What do you think?
Imperatives	Use imperatives or modal verbs to instruct, advise, warn, or recommend readers to do or not do something related to the products or services reviewed	Don't buy this product. You should try this place
Simulated dialogues	Simulate the give and take of an actual conversation, either including both questions and answers or just the answer	"Why do we need to wear masks? Because they protect us and others from getting sick. It's not that hard to understand" (simulated dialogue with a rhetorical question and an answer)
Mentions	Indicate the usernames of other Twitter users to directly address them	@LinguaDigitalis

[2] Note that "we" is a notoriously ambiguous linguistic element and, among other uses, it can be used both in inclusive and exclusive ways.

As mentioned earlier, metadiscourse as an analytical tool has previously been used to explore (academic) writing (e.g. Hyland, 2005, 2017), although more recently the framework has been adapted to explore other genres such as advertising (Al-Subhi, 2022; Fuertes-Olivera et al., 2001), interpersonal interactions (Penz & Marko, 2017), as well as professional (Love et al., 2023), public (Vásquez, 2015), and private social media conversations (Zappavigna, 2018). The application of metadiscourse analysis to online genres is particularly important as it highlights the central role metadiscourse plays in these contexts (Biri, 2021). Through the use of linguistic and discourse resources, writers can effectively "forge a bond" with their readers (Vásquez, 2015: 37), which is a crucial aspect of organisational communication on social media platforms such as Twitter.

In the context of our chapter's focus on organisational identity, metadiscourse analysis serves as a valuable lens for examining the voice of the "organization-as-rhetor". This is because, as Hyland (2005: 3) posits, metadiscourse "embodies the idea that communication is more than just the exchange of information, goods, or services, but also involves the personalities, attitudes, and assumptions of those who are communicating". By analysing metadiscourse in organisational communication, we can gain insights into how an organisation presents itself and relates to its audiences, which are key components of its identity. Metadiscourse analysis thus enables us to identify patterns and variations in the organisation's communicative style, which can provide valuable information about the identity it aims to represent. For example, an organisation that consistently employs a particular metadiscursive strategy in its communication may be signalling a strong, coherent identity, while one that varies its strategies or exhibits inconsistencies may be revealing signs of identity fragmentation. By examining these patterns and their implications, we can better understand the complex interplay between internal and external organisational identity, as well as the potential consequences of identity fragmentation on the organisation's ability to achieve its objectives.

Analysis

Metadiscourse analysis seeks to reveal the ways in which the author of a text engages and involves the reader by focusing on explicit metadiscursive functions. Taxonomies, such as those presented in Tables 6.1 and 6.2 above or in works like Hyland (2005), serve as valuable guides for identifying a range of metadiscourse markers. However, as Ädel (2021) demonstrates, it is essential for the analysis to remain sensitive to the specific text and context under examination. This approach enables the analyst to explore emergent metadiscourse resources in a bottom-up manner, allowing for a richer understanding of the text.

In terms of the actual analysis, this entails conducting a close, interpretative reading of the text, which is informed by, but not restricted to, existing categorisations. By adopting a more flexible approach that allows for the emergence of features, analysts can uncover unique metadiscourse markers that might otherwise be overlooked. This flexibility not only enhances the depth of the analysis but also enables a more nuanced understanding of the ways in which the author of a text communicates with and involves the reader.

Following the first round, close reading directed our attention to the patterns of person-oriented metadiscursive elements, as will be discussed below (Table 6.3).

Self-Mentions

The first pattern that attracted our attention were metadiscourse resources of self-mentions. Self-mentions are crucial in metadiscourse analysis because they draw attention to the writer as a discourse participant (Ädel, 2021). What we see in the analysis is that the different types of self-mentions conceptualise the "self" in three different ways (Table 6.4): either separate from the organisation they represented, part of the entire organisation they represented, or part of a section of the entire organisation.

These discourse resources situate the identities in three different relations to the organisation and therefore the image they communicate to the outside world is ambiguous: the readers are left wondering, for example, if the speaker they represent is either part of the organisation or *is* the organisation itself. This ambiguity at times manifests within a single tweet, for example, "We've set an EVENT target of £250K for the community team who help care at home", where "we" and the "community team" are both part of the same organisation, the hospice, yet the tweet depicts them as two separate entities, projecting multiple (or fragmented) identities of the same organisation. Similar division is created in the tweet "Through Hospice Care Week we'll introduce the unsung heroes of XX Hospice. Behind the scenes they help us go the extra mile", where division is created between the "unsung heroes" and the group

Table 6.3 Tweets over six-month period, anonymised

Date	
08/08	Early Bird tickets are only on sale until the end of August
11/08	All this month Shop will be hosting themes of a retro nature leading up to the Rally on bank holiday weekend. Pop in and see us
13/08	Join the Hospice and Dementia UK in the gardens of Cottage on 21st August…
23/08	Early Bird Tickets are only available for one more week! weblink
27/08	Our Hospice shop on XX Street is having a blue cross sale this Friday and Saturday
12/09	Hospice Fashion Show with style coach XX using donated clothes OCT 7th—£6—at the Club weblink
16/09	Come along and join us at the XX for a coffee morning this Friday at 10am–2 pm The theme of the coffee morning will be—Macmillan
23/09	We are challenging 1000 people to raise £100 by March! weblink
24/09	XX Theatre are hosting an evening of blues and soul in aid of the hospice on the 11th October
30/09	The XX concert is taking place at 7:30 pm on 24th October at the Centre. Tickets are just £5
03/10	Next week is #hospicecareweek. Why not visit the shop & café for a free info pack (stop for cake too if you like)
04/10	Learn more about your Hospice on a tour of the Centre—7th Oct. Call (number) to book #hospicecareweek
05/10	Hospice Fashion Show at Club, (address) with stylist—7th October, doors @ 7 pm Tickets £6 inc glass of bubbly
06/10	Through Hospice Care Week we'll introduce the unsung heroes of XX Hospice. Behind the scenes they help us go the extra mile
07/10	Adel is head of Housekeeping. Part of her role involves working in the on-site laundry weblink
07/10	John is Head Chef at the Hospice and passionate about providing healthy, nutritious meals for patients on the ward weblink
09/10	90% of hospice care in the UK happens away from hospice buildings, this #HospiceCareWeek we're asking you to share your experiences
13/10	XX concert, 24th October, 7.30 pm, XX Centre, £5 entry
14/10	Come along and join us at the centre for a coffee morning this Friday at 10am–2 pm The theme of the coffee morning will be—Breast Cancer
20/10	Santa Dash is back! The 5 km Fun Run takes place in December at the park. Find out more at weblink
21/10	Come along to a XX Night on the 1st November, 7 pm at the Theatre
29/10	T-Shirts & Hoodies SALE!! For Every Item Sold £2 Will Be Donated To The Hospice By weblink
07/11	Santa Run is only one month away! To register for the most festive run of the year visit weblink
18/11	Come along and join us at the Centre for a coffee morning this Friday at 10am–2 pm The theme of the coffee morning will be—Lung and Pancreatic

(continued)

Table 6.3 (continued)

Date	
01/12	Meet the Hospice Minions at Santa Dash this Sunday. For more information visit weblink #minions
16/12	Come along and join us at the Centre for a coffee morning this Friday at 10am–2 pm The theme of the coffee morning will be—Children Illnesses
09/01/	REGISTER for XX event. Celebrate the 25th Anniversary in aid of @XYZ weblink
09/01/	Hi @name—we will have a skydive. Please do email us at info@email.com for more info. Thank you
04/02	In Jan 1,067 people + 76 dogs registered for the EVENT—10th May. Will you join them? weblink
07/02	These Costumes walked 26.5 miles of the EVENT won Best Fancy Dress! Why not join them this year? weblink
10/02	Morning with @name1 to launch the @name2 students promo film for EVENT. Recognise the views? weblink
14/02	Everyone attends the EVENT for different reasons. What's your inspiration? Help inspire others weblink
16/02	We've set an EVENT target of £250K for the community team who help care at home for people at the end of their lives. Register today
21/02	Don't forget you can register your furry friend for EVENT weblink

who introduces them (i.e. the fundraising team), but also "us, who go the extra mile", supposedly the hospice itself. The issue of the social media campaign about "unsung heroes" has previously been discussed extensively in the team, and these discussions provided opportunities for members to lay bare unspoken fractures between the management team, the fundraising team, and the rest of the hospice. It is not surprising, therefore, that this fragmented identity "leaked" into the externally facing communication where the three groups are distinctively constructed in discourse.

Audience Mentions and Engagement Devices

In writing, authors refer to the readers for two reasons: first, to explicitly address them and thus include them as a discourse participant, and second, to rhetorically position them, "pulling readers into the discourse at critical points, predicting possible objections and guiding them to particular interpretations" (Hyland, 2005: 54). Apart from obvious, explicit mentions, interactions with the audience in social media texts is

Table 6.4 Analysis of tweets: self-mentions

Self-mentions	Writer and referenced organisation are separate	All this month Shop will be hosting … Join the Hospice Learn more about your Hospice Donated to the hospice Meet the Hospice Minions
	Writer involvement clearly referring to the hospice as a whole	Our hospice shop
	Reference unclear: organisation as a whole, or income generation team	Pop in and see us Come along and join us We are challenging people We will have a sky dive Email us We'll introduce … help us go the … We're asking you to … We've set the …

often realised through formulaic and idiomatic expression and questions and directives (Vásquez, 2015). Although there seems to be a general understanding that metadiscourse analysis can only work with explicit linguistic manifestations (Ädel, 2021), in our dataset the lack of any such linguistic manifestations, in contrast with the existing ones, will also be considered.

Considering that the primary goals of the fundraising team are to encourage participation in fundraising events and donations to the hospice, in their tweets there is a startling lack of direct engagement with their audience (Table 6.5). The tweets we labelled "Exclusion of the audience" are a case in point: these serve as announcements with no effort to directly address or explicitly engage readers; it is, we suspect, simply assumed that an imagined audience will consider these announcements as relevant. This hypothesis is supported by the fact that the announcement tweets contain specifics about the events, including place, time, and price. Nonetheless, these tweets project a level of formality or authority by avoiding direct engagement with the audience. They avoid interactivity

Table 6.5 Analysis of tweets: audience engagement

Audience engagement	Direct references to the audience	we're asking you to share your experiences Learn more about your Hospice Will you join them? What's your inspiration? Don't forget you can register your furry friend Hi @name	
	Indirect references to the audience	Indirect mentions	We are challenging 1000 people Help inspire others
		Directives	Join the Hospice Come along and join us (3x) Find out more at weblink To register... (3x) Meet the Hospice Minions Celebrate the 25th anniversary
		Questions	Why not visit the shop Why not join them this year? Recognise the views?
	Exclusion of the audience	T-Shirts & Hoodies SALE!! Early Bird tickets are on sale (2x) Our Hospice shop on XX Street is having a blue cross sale Hospice Fashion Show with style coach XX Theatre are hosting an evening The XX concert is taking place Hospice Fashion Show at Club Through Hospice Care Week we'll introduce XX concert, 24th October, 7.30 pm, XX Centre, £5 entry	

and lead to a one-sided communication dynamic. Even though directives are considered to be devices to engage readers, considering the formulaic and repetitive nature of the ones identified in the tweets, and the fact that these are calls for action to "join", "register", "find out more", and "come along", these further contribute to the image of a detached and unapproachable organisation.

The five questions we identified in the tweets create a better interactional relationship, because questions typically position readers as active participants in the discourse (see Vásquez, 2015: 30). However, while rhetorical questions are present in some of the tweets, the low frequency of questions (only five out of 34 tweets) may project an image that the organisation does not consistently engage with its audience or actively seek their input. The omission of the grammatical subject in three of the tweets ("Why not …?" "Recognise the views?") might be an effort to avoid directly addressing the audience, creating a sense of ambiguity and distance. Regarding the questions observed, another noteworthy point is the pattern in which they occur. For instance, no questions were posted before February, but after February all tweets contained a question. Such a cluster of features might suggest that a new member took over the management of the social media feed, and in the absence of a coherent organisational voice, they relied on their personal style of tweeting.

Observations and Discussion

In his seminal work, Hyland (2005: 49) attests that person-oriented metadiscourse is "the writer's expression of a textual 'voice' or community-recognised personality". But what happens if the "writer" speaks in different voices and displays not one but several personalities? This question is crucial when the "writer" is an organisation—as is the case in external corporate communication. External corporate communication has previously attracted the attention of scholars exploring organisational identity because, on the one hand, it is a site where organisations can actively manage perceptions about their identity (Fombrun & Rindova, 2000), or, on the other and, a context where organisational identities are contested and negotiated between the public and the members of the organisation (Coupland & Brown, 2004). In this chapter, we have taken a different approach and, using metadiscourse analysis, we set out to expose the "voice" and "personality" of the organisation-as-rhetor in social media posts.

Our analysis of Twitter data from the hospice revealed two main issues: ambiguity of self-mentions and limited engagement with the addressed audiences. The metadiscourse resources of self-mentions (Table 6.4) revealed that the tweets conceptualise the "self" in three distinct ways, thus creating a perception for the audiences that the organisation speaks in three distinct voices. This ambiguity is even observed within single messages, projecting multiple or fragmented identities of the same organisation. If we consider this in the broader context of the problems our fundraising team faced at the time of the restructuring, this fragmentation in the communication is symptomatic of the lack of shared values and beliefs and unclear common goals within the hospice. In our analyses of the criticism levelled at the management team in Chapter 5, we have already noted this malaise. The analysis of metadiscourse resources that typically create opportunities for audience engagement (Table 6.5) highlights the lack of effort to connect with audiences and even a lack of acknowledgement of their existence. This is particularly problematic in the current communicative environment where interactivity on social media is considered to be crucial for the success of an organisation's communication efforts (Rogala, 2016)—and for our hospice income generation team, these efforts would ensure the success of fundraising initiatives, from encouraging participation in fundraising events to encouraging donations to the hospice. The lack of explicit addressee mentions, the low frequency of questions, the omission of the grammatical subject, and the formulaic nature of directives contribute to the image of a detached and unapproachable organisation (cf. Koller & Ereaut, 2020). The patterns of occurrence of various discourse features and the inconsistencies in both self-mentions and audience engagement devices suggest that the organisation lacks a coherent voice in its external communication, and this may have adversely affected its credibility and overall image. Indeed, one of the key outcomes of the consultancy revealed that before addressing communication issues on social media, the team—and the entire organisation—needed to address problems arising from their fragmented identity (Darics, 2020).

Conclusions for Research and Practice

Organisational identity is not only a well-researched theoretical construct but inextricably linked to the outcome of organisational efforts. The inward-facing aspect of organisational identity is critical for building a strong and cohesive organisational culture. This includes developing a shared sense of purpose, values, and beliefs among employees, as well as aligning individual and organisational goals. By cultivating a positive organisational identity, employees feel a sense of belonging and are motivated to work towards achieving the organisation's objectives (Dutton et al., 1994; Harrison, 2000; Madsen, 2016). The outward-facing aspect of organisational identity is equally important, as it influences stakeholder perceptions and relationships. A strong and positive organisational identity can enhance reputation, build trust and credibility, and increase loyalty among customers and investors. By projecting a clear and consistent identity to the outside world, organisations can attract new customers and retain existing ones, as well as attract investors and other stakeholders (Fombrun & Rindova, 2000; Rogala, 2016).

This is the ideal situation. However, as we have discussed earlier, identities are social constructions, constantly challenged, (re)negotiated, and (re)established, as people in an organisation respond to changes and challenges, whether these have been brought on by an organisational restructuring (Mills et al., 2005), controversial societal issues (Henderson et al., 2015), or simply by the affordance of evolving social media communication (Cheney & Christensen, 2001). Organisational members, as we have seen in the previous chapters, make sense of their realities in multiple ways (cf. Harrison, 2000). What if, as He and Brown (2013: 11) ask, "this leads to a realization that organizations have as many identities as they have members?"

Whether this is the case or not, organisations cannot function successfully without a shared understanding of what they stand for and where they intend to go. Communicating this understanding both within the walls of the organisation and towards the outside world is crucial to achieving the organisation's purpose, and to do this, they must continuously monitor, evaluate, and adapt their communication strategies. This work starts by raising awareness of the potential impact that external communication can have on both internal and external stakeholder perceptions. It requires an ongoing reflection and awareness of the evolving nature of organisational identity and communication practices.

Implementing the goal of effectively managing organisational identity has been a significant topic of research, as evidenced by the extensive body of scholarship reviewed in this chapter and beyond. In our study, we have introduced metadiscourse analysis as a valuable tool for examining social media content, highlighting its capacity to uncover the complexities of organisational identity construction. By focusing not only on the content of communication but also on the ways in which social media messages engage the audience, we have been able to investigate the "voice" of the organisation and the identity it conveys. Although our findings suggest a somewhat fragmented identity and incoherent organisational voice for the hospice, another perspective may offer a more optimistic view: the examination of the (strength of) team spirit in the next chapter.

References

Ädel, A. (2021). Reflections on reflexivity in digital communication: Towards a third wave of metadiscourse studies. In L. D'Angelo, A. Mauranen, & S. Maci (Eds.), *Metadiscourse in digital communication: New research, approaches and methodologies* (pp. 37–64). Springer.

Al-Subhi, A. S. (2022). Metadiscourse in online advertising: Exploring linguistic and visual metadiscourse in social media advertisements. *Journal of Pragmatics, 187*, 24–40.

Albert, S., Ashforth, B. E., & Dutton, J. E. (2000). Organizational identity and identification: Charting new waters and building new bridges. *Academy of Management Review, 25*(1), 13–17.

Alvesson, M. (1994). Talking in organizations: Managing identity and impressions in an advertising agency. *Organization Studies, 15*(4), 535–563.

Angouri, J., & Marra, M. (Eds.). (2011). *Constructing identities at work.* Springer.

Biri, Y. (2021). Metadiscourse in social media: A reflexive framework. In L. D'Angelo, A. Mauranen, & S. Maci (Eds.), *Metadiscourse in digital communication: New research, approaches and methodologies* (pp. 133–154). Springer.

Brown, A. D. (2015). Identities and identity work in organizations. *International Journal of Management Reviews, 17*(1), 20–40.

Bucholtz, M., & Hall, K. (2005). Identity and interaction: A sociocultural linguistic approach. *Discourse Studies, 7*(4–5), 585–614.

Cheney, G., & Christensen, L. (2001). Organizational identity: Linkages between internal and external communication. In F. M. Jablin & L. L. Putnam (Eds.), *The new handbook of organizational communication* (pp. 231–270). Sage.

Cornelissen, J. P., Haslam, S. A., & Balmer, J. M. (2007). Social identity, organizational identity and corporate identity: Towards an integrated understanding of processes, patternings and products. *British Journal of Management, 18*, S1–S16.

Coupland, C., & Brown, A. D. (2004). Constructing organizational identities on the web: A case study of Royal Dutch/Shell. *Journal of Management Studies, 41*(8), 1325–1347.

D'Angelo, L., Mauranen, A., & Maci, S. (Eds.). (2021). *Metadiscourse in digital communication: New research, approaches and methodologies.* Springer Nature.

Darics, E. (2015). Digital media in workplace interactions. In A. Georgakopoulou & T. Spilioti (Eds.), *The Routledge handbook of language and digital communication* (pp. 197–211). Routledge.

Darics, E. (2020). The relevance of applied linguistic and discourse research: On the margins of communication consultancy. In L. Mullany (Ed.), *Professional communication: Consultancy, advocacy, activism* (pp. 47–64). Palgrave.

Di Lauro, S., Tursunbayeva, A., Antonelli, G., & Martinez, M. (2020). Organizational and corporate identity on social media: A literature review. *International Journal of Business and Management, 15*(4), 1–53.

Dutton, J. E., Dukerich, J. M., & Harquail, C. V. (1994). Organizational images and member identification. *Administrative Science Quarterly, 39*, 239–263.

Elsbach, K. D., & Kramer, R. M. (1996). Members' responses to organizational identity threats: Encountering and countering the Business Week rankings. *Administrative Science Quarterly, 41*, 442–476.

Fombrun, C., & Rindova, V. (2000). The road to transparency: Reputation management at Royal/Dutch Shell. In M. Schultz, M. J. Hatch, & M. Holten Larsen (Eds.), *The expressive organization: Linking identity, reputation and the corporate brand* (pp. 7–96). Oxford University Press.

Fuertes-Olivera, P. A., Velasco-Sacristán, M., Arribas-Baño, A., & Samaniego-Fernández, E. (2001). Persuasion and advertising English: Metadiscourse in slogans and headlines. *Journal of pragmatics, 33*(8), 1291–1307.

Harrison, J. D. (2000). Multiple imaginings of institutional identity: A case study of a large psychiatric research hospital. *The Journal of Applied Behavioral Science, 36*(4), 425–455.

He, H., & Brown, A. D. (2013). Organizational identity and organizational identification: A review of the literature and suggestions for future research. *Group & Organization Management, 38*(1), 3–35.

Henderson, A., Cheney, G., & Weaver, C. K. (2015). The role of employee identification and organizational identity in strategic communication and organizational issues management about genetic modification. *International Journal of Business Communication, 52*(1), 12–41.

Hyland, K. (2005). *Metadiscourse: Exploring interaction in writing*. Bloomsbury Publishing.

Hyland, K. (2017). Metadiscourse: What is it and where is it going? *Journal of Pragmatics, 113*, 16–29.

Jameson, D. A. (2014). Crossing public-private and personal-professional boundaries: How changes in technology may affect CEOs' communication. *Business and Professional Communication Quarterly, 77*(1), 7–30.

Kjærgaard, A. L. (2009). Organizational identity and strategy: An empirical study of organizational identity's influence on the strategy-making process. *International Studies of Management & Organization, 39*(1), 50–69.

Koller, V., & Ereaut, G. (2020). Culture change and rebranding in the charity sector: A linguistic consultancy approach. In L. Mullany (Ed.), *Professional communication: Consultancy, advocacy, activism* (pp. 89–111). Palgrave.

Love, R., Darics, E., & Palmieri, R. (2023). Engaging the public: English local government organisations' social media communications during the COVID-19 pandemic. *Applied Corpus Linguistics*, 100060.

Madsen, V. T. (2016). Constructing organizational identity on internal social media: A case study of coworker communication in Jyske Bank. *International Journal of Business Communication, 53*(2), 200–223.

Mills, M., Bettis, P., Miller, J. W., & Nolan, R. (2005). Experiences of academic unit reorganization: Organizational identity and identification in organizational change. *The Review of Higher Education, 28*(4), 597–619.

Penz, H., & Marko, G. (2017). Metadiscourse in interactive contexts: An introduction. *AAA: Arbeiten aus Anglistik und Amerikanistik* [Papers from English and American Studies], *42*(2), 185–188.

Ravasi, D., & Canato, A. (2013). How do I know who you think you are? A review of research methods on organizational identity. *International Journal of Management Reviews, 15*(2), 185–204.

Ravasi, D., & Van Rekom, J. (2003). Key issues in organizational identity and identification theory. *Corporate Reputation Review, 6*, 118–132.

Rogala, A. (2016). The dependencies between internal and external communication of the organization: The problem of coherence. In *Entrepreneurship, Business and Economics-Vol. 1: Proceedings of the 15th Eurasia Business and Economics Society Conference* (pp. 485–500). Springer.

Sillince, J. A., & Brown, A. D. (2009). Multiple organizational identities and legitimacy: The rhetoric of police websites. *Human Relations, 62*(12), 1829–1856.

Sveningsson, S., & Alvesson, M. (2003). Managing managerial identities: Organizational fragmentation, discourse and identity struggle. *Human Relations, 56*(10), 1163–1193.

Van De Mieroop, D., & Schnurr, S. (Eds.). (2017). *Identity struggles: Evidence from workplaces around the world* (Vol. 69). John Benjamins Publishing Company.

Vásquez, C. (2015). 'Don't even get me started...': Interactive metadiscourse in online consumer reviews. In E. Darics (Ed.), *Digital business discourse* (pp. 19–39). Palgrave.

Whetten, D. A. (2006). Albert and Whetten revisited: Strengthening the concept of organizational identity. *Journal of Management Inquiry, 15*(3), 219–234.

Zappavigna, M. (2018). *Searchable talk: Hashtags and social media metadiscourse.* Bloomsbury Publishing

CHAPTER 7

Conversation Analysis, Enacting Teams, and Displaying Team Spirit in a Decision-Making Episode of Talk

Introduction

Teams are said to be a key part of post-bureaucratic organisations with flatter and more consultative hierarchies (Levi, 2015). Consequently, they have long been the focus of both academic work (e.g. Cohen & Bailey, 1997; Kozlowski & Bell, 2003; Levi, 2015) and more popular management "how-to" books (e.g. Brounstein, 2009; Hamilton, 2021). However, the notion of team spirit, often assumed to be an important ingredient of high-performing teams, has generated less academic attention compared to the more popular management "how-to" books which have no qualms about announcing that they have found the elusive pot of gold at the end of the rainbow and can reduce team spirit to wish lists of behaviours. To our knowledge, no research has so far used transcripts of naturally occurring interaction of a team in action to analyse just what it is about the team's interaction that enacts something as apparently vague, and "impossible to qualify", as team spirit (Silva et al., 2014: 287). To address this lacuna, we use conversation analysis (henceforth CA) to analyse the funding team's interaction as they go about a mundane workplace activity of making a decision, and we attempt to locate the phenomenon of "team spirit" in sequences of talk. To make visible, and thus analysable, the enactment of team spirit as it actually occurs in real time, we particularly make use of CA's notion of affiliation, whereby

E. Darics and J. Clifton, *Organisation, Communication and Language*, New Perspectives in Organizational Communication,
https://doi.org/10.1007/978-3-031-30199-5_7

participants not only respond to each other's talk but do so in a maximally pro-social way by, at an affective level, matching the prior speaker's evaluative stance and displaying empathy and/or cooperation with the prior action (Stivers et al., 2011: 21).

This chapter is structured as follows. First, we review the literature on teams and team spirit in both academic and popular management literature. We then introduce you to CA as a research methodology and suggest how it can be used to make teamwork and more specifically team spirit visible, and thus analysable. After this, we analyse a real-time decision-making episode of talk and highlight how a team is talked into being and how team spirit is enacted. In the final section, we address how the findings of this analysis can complement both organisational research into teams and how it can be of value and interest to practitioners.

Teams and Team Spirit

The steady rise of teams to prominence in the organisational landscape has been a result of the move away from top-down hierarchical management, in which the manager alone traditionally had both the social position and expertise to direct the workforce, to flatter hierarchies and collective decision-making that is characteristic of post-bureaucratic organisations. Teams, while not being without their critics (e.g. Sinclair, 1992), are said to be essential to improving the quality of an organisation's products and services, and they are therefore a vital factor in contributing to organisational success (Levi, 2015: 9). Considering their importance to organisations and organising, teams have been at the centre of considerable academic research.

This work has both focused on team types, such as top management teams (Aboramadan, 2021) or virtual teams (Hertel et al., 2005), and phenomena related to teams, such as trust (Costa, 2003), leadership (Day et al., 2004), and decision-making (Abatecola et al., 2013). Conversely, team spirit has received relatively little research interest. As Ratzmann et al. (2018) and Silva et al. (2014) point out, its presence is often assumed rather than investigated. A further explanation for the lack of research into team spirit per se may be because it has an "impossible-to-qualify quality element" to it that is made up of "invisible ingredients whose presence people feel, yet are often unable to define properly or formally acknowledge" (Silva et al., 2014: 288).

Further, most scholarly research that has investigated the notion of team spirit has done so using interviews and surveys that have either analysed what team players perceive team spirit to be (e.g. Silva et al., 2014) or, working from a priori definitions of team spirit, have sought to measure it and assess its role in team performance (see, for example, Jawoski & Kohli, 1993; Ratzmann et al., 2018; Salojärvi & Saarenketo, 2013). Of the surveyed literature, only one paper (Pentland, 2012) claimed to have located team spirit in the actual behaviour of teams. The data from which Pentland (2012) claimed to have identified team spirit were collected by "electronic badges" which monitored and "measured" the communicative behaviour of team members for such phenomena as "the tone of voice, body language, whom they talked to and how much, and more" (Pentland, 2012: 4). However, despite claims to be able to locate team spirit in people's communicative behaviour, the exact details of this behaviour were vague and unreported. This research, by culminating in a promise to improve individual and team performance if one follows three simple steps, resonates with non-academic work on team spirit designed for practitioners. For example, Heerman (2003), working from an anecdotal definition of team spirit, which he defines as a "committed exploration for meaning and purpose in life and work" (Heerman, 2003: 41), gives advice on how to achieve this in a six-stage process. Similar advice is found on various websites, blogs, and so on. For example, Rabha (no date), working from a dictionary definition, offers advice on how team spirit can be achieved through, inter alia, practising problem-solving skills, organising team lunches and events, and establishing communication flow. However, the nitty-gritty of how one actually establishes "communication flow", or how exactly a lunch can establish team spirit, is not provided.

In short, while teams and, to a lesser extent, team spirit have been the focus of much prior research, little, if any, academic research has used transcripts of naturally occurring team interaction to attempt to locate such an ephemeral phenomenon as team spirit. Conversely, practitioner-oriented literature is generally not shy about proclaiming that it knows both what team spirit is and how to obtain it, provided practitioners follow the advice it gives. While no doubt many of the writers of such literature have significant experience in managing teams, their advice is based on anecdotal evidence and not on direct observation of what actually goes on during team interaction. The purpose of this chapter is, therefore, using CA as a methodological tool, to analyse extracts of naturally occurring team talk in order to make visible how teams are enacted in talk and how team spirit is achieved as an interactional accomplishment. We then consider the usefulness of such insights to practitioners in terms of raising awareness of how a team "does" team spirit in real-time, in situ practice.

Method: Conversation Analysis (CA)

It is beyond the scope of this chapter to provide an in-depth summary of conversation analysis (CA). You can have a look at the numerous monographs, for example, Hutchby and Wooffitt (2008), Sidnell and Stivers (2013), and ten Have (2007), that already amply do this. Suffice to say that CA was developed by Harvey Sacks and colleagues (notably Gail Jefferson and Emmanuel Schegloff) in California in the 1960s. Sacks died tragically in 1975, having published relatively little during his lifetime. However, his lectures (Sacks, 1992) were transcribed by Gail Jefferson and published posthumously in 1992, and his work has now developed into a well-known field of inquiry. Antaki (2011: 1) sums up this body of research as "the study of how social action is brought about through the close organisation of talk", which is to say that CA pays particular attention to both sequences of talk and the action, or actions, that these sequences of talk perform. In order to analyse how social action is achieved in talk, the *sine qua non* of CA is the use of recordings of naturally occurring talk. Traditionally, these recordings have been audio, but since the arrival of good and cheap video-recording material, CA has begun to investigate the multimodal achievement of social action and researchers have been paying increasing attention to the sequential importance of gesture, space, and material objects in interaction (for more on this see Deppermann, 2013). However, because the data for this book were collected by the use of microphones which the participants carried with them throughout the working day, in this chapter we limit ourselves to the transcripts of audio recordings.

Once you have recordings, whether video or audio, of naturally occurring interaction, you then need to meticulously transcribe them and use these transcriptions to make visible, and thus analysable, how actions such as blaming, complaining, arguing, teamwork, and so on are achieved through sequences of talk. Essential to such analyses is the refusal to initiate analyses based on researchers' a priori hypotheses as to what might be going on. Rather, the analyses of the transcripts are based on analysing sequences in talk in which the participants' understanding of a prior turn is displayed in the following talk (the next turn proof procedure [Sacks et al., 1974: 728]). Through this procedure, you can base your analyses on how the next speakers respond to prior turns in talk and how they display their understandings of prior turns at talk. Such displayed understandings are also available to researchers who are able to understand what is demonstrably "going on" through their own membership knowledge (Peräkylä, 2011: 369). Therefore, if in response to the turn "Hello, how are you?" one replies "I am fine, thanks", then it is observable that the participants are doing a greeting. However, if the reply is "Well, actually I've got a bit of a pain in my stomach", then it could be that the participants are doing a medical encounter. In short, any CA analysis has to be anchored in the displayed orientations of the participants themselves, and so researcher a priori hypotheses as to what is significant for the participants are avoided.

More specifically, in line with the focus of this chapter, there is a wealth of research which deals with multiparty/team interaction from a CA perspective, some of which particularly focuses on organisational settings (e.g. Boden, 1994; Nielsen, 2009; Svennevig, 2012). Further, as Sacks et al. (1974) point out, the organisation of turn-taking is related not to individuals but to parties in talk which are formed "by virtue of interaction-specific contingencies of conduct" (Schegloff, 1995: 33). Thus, as Lerner (1993) notes, if a couple goes into a restaurant, they may be oriented to as a single party and either of the couple may speak on behalf of the other, so establishing the relevance of a single party to talk. Parties in talk, therefore, may be created and sustained by:

- speaking to recipients as an association;
- speaking for and as an association;
- one member speaking to another member as an association;
- speaking about an association of participants. (Lerner, 1993: 220)

Associations are, therefore, talked into being in and through the sequential properties of talk and such actions as co-authoring or otherwise sharing, continuing, repeating, and/or completing turns at talk (see, for example, Djordjilovic, 2012; Gordon, 2003; Kangasharju, 1996, 2002;

Lerner, 1993; Sacks, 1992: Vol. 1: 145). Consequently, from this perspective, a team, rather than being a pre-discursive entity, is an interactional achievement. As (Djordjilovic, 2012: 113), building on Kangasharju (1996: 292), puts it:

> teams are characterized by the fact that participants explicitly act as an association by making this association visible to other participants. Such interactional teams are made visible through the way in which turns are co-constructed and speaking rights are managed; participants affiliate at an affective level, and align at a sequential level; and participants realize shared accountability and authorship of the action in progress.

From such an interactional perspective, teams have been the focus of many CA studies (e.g. Clifton, 2014; Djordjilovic, 2012; Housley, 2000). However, to date none of these studies have, to our knowledge, sought to go beyond analysing teamwork and the formation of teams to look at team spirit. In order to build on prior CA work on teamwork, we pay particular attention to the notion of affiliation which has, as Lindström and Sorjonen (2013: 364) suggest, so far been under-researched in CA-oriented work on group dynamics—though see Marakaki et al. (2010) who analyse laugher in a team setting. Broadly, we argue that, in order for team talk to progress and for team objectives to be achieved, alignment (i.e. structural cooperation) is necessary, yet for team spirit to be achieved, affiliation (i.e. affective cooperation), which is maximally pro-social (Stivers et al., 2011: 21), must also be realised.

Alignment is achieved when, in subsequent turns at talk, participants display their acceptance of the presuppositions and terms of any proposed action and facilitate its achievement (Stivers et al., 2011: 20). Expanding on this observation, and paraphrasing Oittinen (2018: 34), we note that alignment is about supporting the action, or turn in progress, establishing mutual understanding (intersubjectivity) and accepting identities made relevant in the talk (e.g. speaker/hearer, chair/participants, manager/subordinate, etc.). Conversely, disalignment is an action, such as topic shift, that interferes with the activity in progress. Affiliation, on the other hand, displays preference, empathy, and supports the prior speaker's stance (i.e. the displayed affective attitude to the action in progress). Disaffiliation is therefore an action that rejects the prior speaker's stance. Several observations are worth making about the relation between affiliative and aligning turns at talk. First, turns are not necessarily constituted *solely* of talk, and thus displays of affiliation and alignment may involve, or be constituted entirely of, laughter, clapping, gaze, manipulation of artefacts, body position, and so on. Second, whereas aligning turns are expected, affiliative turns are not. Thus, as Stivers et al. (2011: 21) point out, a request such as "Where is the elevator?" projects alignment as a next action (e.g. "it's over there" or even "sorry, I don't know"), but it would not project affiliation. Third, a disaligning response may be affiliative. For example, one may interrupt a story in progress and so do disalignment, but such a turn may still be affiliative by supporting the storyteller's stance. Fourth, affiliation and alignment are closely linked to the notion of preference[1] (Lee & Tanaka, 2016: 2). This is because, as Pomerantz (1984: 55) points out, the design/shape of preferred/dispreferred actions is used to maximise cooperation and affiliation and to minimise conflict.

Returning to this chapter's objective (i.e. making visible and thus analysable the doing of teams and team spirit), in the following section we analyse a decision-making episode of talk drawn from our corpus and draw out what makes this team talk. To do this, returning to Djordjilovic's (2012) definition of teamwork, we pay particular attention to how participants manage speaking rights and co-construct turns; affiliate at an affective level, and align at a sequential level; and realise shared accountability and authorship of the action in progress. Further, arguing that if team spirit does indeed exist it is locatable in interaction, we particularly investigate the talk for evidence of maximally pro-social behaviour between participants that not only talks the team into being but which does so in a way that makes team spirit (conceptualised as doing acts of affiliation) visible, and thus analysable, in talk. However, as discussed in more detail later, we do not claim that affiliation necessarily equates with team spirit; rather, we suggest that when clusters of affiliative actions occur, team spirit may be present.

Such a researcher-driven linking of a CA analysis of affiliation and the notion of team spirit of course runs the risk of supplanting the participants' own orientation to phenomena such as affiliation with the researcher's interest in team spirit. However, Drew (2005: 99) notes that "it might be misdealing to suggest that there is one methodology, when

[1] Preference in CA relates to the structural preference in sequences of talk for some types of turn design over others. For example, second turns which do agreement are preferred over turns that do disagreement. For more on preference, see Pomerantz (1984).

in reality there are certain differences and diversities in the ways in which conversation analysts work". Therefore, in this chapter, we take what Seedhouse (2005: 180) describes as a "CA-informed" or "CA-inspired" approach to analysis, as opposed to a "purist" or "hardcore" approach. In other words, while using the language and technology of CA to investigate the sequential properties of talk in naturally occurring interaction, by drawing on the a priori notion of team spirit, we are clearly ***drawing on*** CA to answer a non-CA question (see Clifton and Rømer Barfod [forthcoming] for a finer discussion of the implications of using CA for non-CA purposes).

Conversation Analysis and Team Spirit

In what follows, we showcase how CA can be used to gain insights into something as intangible as "team spirit". First, in line with the core tenets of CA, this requires "unmotivated looking", which means that rather than having an a priori idea of what we want to look at, we work from "something of interest" that emerges from the repeated listening to the recordings as we are transcribing. This avoids a priori research interests skewing the analysis to what the researcher is looking for. As Sacks (1984: 25) stated: "when we start out with a piece of data, the question of what we are going to end up with, what kind of findings it will give, should not be a consideration. We sit down with a piece of data, make a bunch of observations and then see where they will go".

In this case, team spirit was not an issue we set out to investigate. Rather, on listening to this particular meeting, we were struck by the amount of laughter and "banter". Consequently, we sought to answer the classic CA question: why this now? In other words, why is this particular turn designed in this particular way, at this particular moment, and what social action does it achieve? The "bunch of observations" we made were of course guided by the existing body of CA scholarship that can be brought to focus on what actions are being achieved and how. This case study was particularly guided by CA work on laughter in interaction (e.g. Glenn, 1991, 2003; Jefferson et al., 1987), which counter-intuitively doesn't write off laughter as something that is either necessarily linked to humour or as something that is non-serious and therefore irrelevant for interaction and organisations. After doing the analyses, zooming out from the interactional achievement of the team and the sequential properties of talk to team spirit is something that many CA scholars would be reluctant to do. This is because "team spirit" is a researcher's concern rather than something that the participants are demonstrably orienting to. However, concurring with Ford (2012: 508) who argues that "CA is simply too powerful an approach to be abandoned because one is not using it in service of its own primary end" (i.e. the local practices of turn-taking and the sequential organisation of talk per se), we link the CA-inspired analyses of the interaction to the wider organisational phenomenon of "team spirit". Consequently, we apply and adapt CA to a non-CA research agenda in the hope of providing insights into organisational phenomena that other methods of analysis may not be able to provide. However, at the same time as zooming out, any claims that we make are still anchored in, and warranted by, fine-grained analysis of the interaction.

Analysis

In this chapter, we focus on a decision-making episode in talk in which the fundraising team are discussing which events to publicise in the local press. The meeting involves Amy, Victoria, Lisa, Dot, and Kira. Victoria and Lisa are not members of the fundraising team; they are volunteers. Our analyses focus on the suggestion and final decision to put Funky Peach's fundraising event, in which she will cut her hair and donate it to a wig maker, in the local press. Following Huisman (2001), decisions are formulations of a current (problematic) state of affairs and a commitment to future action to resolve a "problematic" situation. Therefore, in this analysis we investigate a decision-making episode of talk in which a "problem" (which fundraising event to put in the local press) is formulated and a solution (to include Funky Peach's event) is suggested and finally accepted. We argue that it is in and through such mundane talk that a team is enacted and team spirit is achieved.

Extract 7.1: Locating the Problem

In the talk immediately prior to Extract 7.1, the participants have been suggesting events that could be publicised in the local press. We join the interaction when Kira introduces the topic of a local singer-songwriter's fundraising activity as a possible event to include in the press.

Extract 7.1

1.	Kira	erm (.) we got er (.) Funky Peach↑
2.	Amy	Funky↓
3.	Kira	yeah
4.	Amy	we = we're banking quite a lot on Funky
5.	Dot	Funky (.) the only thing is she's donating her hair to a wig maker
6.	Amy	yeah
7.	Kira	which-we've gotta find a wig maker (.) which we're already down the
8.		route er Judith has replied with some people and so has Liz and so has Cliff

In line 1, Kira introduces the topic of Funky Peach, the singer-songwriter. Significantly, she uses the pronoun "we", which, through speaking on behalf of an association (i.e. in this case the fundraising team), makes that team relevant to the interaction (Gordon, 2003; Kangasharju, 1996; Lerner, 1993). In line 4, Amy assesses the fundraising event as implicitly problematic because they are "banking quite a lot on Funky". A second assessment that aligns and affiliates with this thus becomes a preferred next action (Pomerantz, 1984). In this case, prefacing her turn with "the only thing is", which is hearable as suggesting a problem, Dot aligns and affiliates with Amy's assessment. She also upgrades the assessment by providing the reason for the problematic nature of the event, which is because "she's donating her hair to a wig maker" (line 5). In line six, Amy acknowledges this and aligns with Dot ("yeah"). However, in line 7, Kira adds an increment ("which-we've gotta find a wig maker") to Dot's prior turn. Increments, as Ford et al. (2002: 16) define them, are non-main clauses that continue the prior turn after a possible point of turn completion. In other words, Dot's turn "the only thing is she's donating her hair to a wig maker" which projects a problem is completed by Kira who specifies the problem "which-we've gotta find a wig maker". In this way, Dot and Kira co-author a turn at talk which both displays that they are a team (Lerner, 1993; Sacks, 1992, Vol. 1: 322) and continues the action projected by the prior turn (i.e. defining the problem with Funky's contribution). Kira thus both aligns and affiliates with Dot (and before that Amy) by displaying, and co-authoring, the same stance, i.e. that there is something problematic about Funky's charity event. In sum, through co-authoring this stance, Dot, Amy, and Kira act as a team, and since they also affiliate by sharing the same affective stance, they also potentially make visible team spirit in action. Although, as pointed out previously, we consider team spirit to be enacted where there is a cluster of affiliating actions, rather than just one. In the continuation of the analyses, we highlight the development of this cluster of affiliative actions and so the enactment of "team spirit".

Extract 7.2: Making a Suggestion

In Extract 7.2, there is little evidence of affiliation; rather, Dot minimally aligns with Amy's turn and so moves the talk forward, but without any displays of affiliation—thus, it is difficult to claim in this brief extract that team spirit is enacted. However, this talk is essential to the decision-making and for this reason, it is still analysed.

Extract 7.2

9.	Amy	okay so:::↓ do you think because we have to come up with
10.		something on Monday (.) that if (name on newspaper) like it we could (.)
11.		have her next Friday saying she's going to do it so there's
12.		picture of her [with the story and then
13.	Dot	[yeah
14.	Amy	the following Friday (.) or following Monday Tuesday she does
15.		it and they come and take a photo of her
16.	Dot	yeah

In the continuation of the talk, Amy formulates the upshot of the prior talk as a proposal to put Funky's fundraising event in the local press. Dot aligns with this suggestion as it is in progress (line 13: "yeah") and self-selects at the end of Amy's turn to "do" agreement (line 16: "yeah") with Amy's proposal. Dot thus aligns with the suggestion, but she does not display any particular affiliation other than minimally agreeing with the suggestion. Significantly, as noted in the analysis of Extract 7.1, Amy continues using the collective "we" (lines 9 and 10), thus orienting to finding a solution to the issue of which charity event to place in the local press as a collective issue. This, therefore, again (cf. lines 1, 4, and 7) makes the collective "fundraising team" relevant for the talk.

Extract 7.3: Teasing and Team Spirit

In the following extract, talk deviates from the decision-making talk and there is a short teasing incident which leads to collective laughter and, we argue, a display that the participants share the same stance. Collective laughter is, as Marakaki et al. (2010: 1527) argue, one way of achieving affiliation and "doing" being a team. Indeed, it is one of the few activities in which the "one at a time" rule of turn-taking is suspended so that all participants are potentially implicated in the same action at the same time (Sacks, 1992: 745). However, it is noticeable that this aside has little to do with the task in hand of decision-making, and so while affiliation is displayed, the decision-making talk is put on hold.

Extract 7.3

17.	Amy	yeah↑ would you ask her
18.	Lisa	has she = has she got long hair
19.		(.2)
20.		has she got quite a lot of hair
21.	Dot	yeah
22.	Lisa	okay
23.	Amy	she's healthy
24.	Lisa	so that'd be quite [( )
25.	Dot	[£ye::s£
26.	Amy	she's not got really short hair he heuh
27.	Lisa	as long hi hi as she's not hi got a crew cut hh hi
28.		((general laughter))
29.	Kira	erm we could use Kelly Smith erm who's in the pic during the challenge
30.		1,000 that = that'd be a nice picture

In line 17, after agreeing with the proposal to include Funky Peach's event in the press, Amy asks Dot to "ask her" (i.e. to ask Funky to do the charity event on the following Friday, Monday, or Tuesday). However, disaligning with this turn, Lisa asks: "has she [i.e. Funky] got long hair". There is then a slight pause in which there is no uptake, and so Lisa reformulates her question: "has she got quite a lot of hair". Dot aligns with this question ("yeah") and Lisa acknowledges the response (line 22: "okay"). In line 25 ("she's healthy"), Amy self-selects to also respond to Lisa's question. The utterance "she's healthy" sets up a tease (Drew, 1987). This is because in response to the question about the length and quantity of Funky's hair, Amy chooses an adjective that is exaggerated and extreme, which displays its ironic content. Amy, therefore, orients to the question about Funky's hair as in some way overdone and, in this case, unnecessary or misplaced. However, Lisa does not display recognition of "she's healthy" as ironic and potentially teasing; rather, she begins a turn that projects a serious upshot of the fact that Funky has a lot of long and healthy hair (line 26: "so that'd be quite"). As the turn is in progress, and before an upshot is announced, Dot utters "yes" in a smile voice (i.e. an utterance spoken in "a markedly higher pitch and an intonational contour comparable to laughing during speaking but without any laughter tokens" [Buttny, 2001: 317]). Considering its position, the "yes" refers back to, and aligns with, Amy's (exaggerated) assessment that Funky is healthy. The smile voice therefore projects that Dot recognises the assessment as a tease, and so affiliates with Amy by showing the same stance. In the following turn, Amy extends the emerging tease by answering the question again (line 28: "she's not got really short hair he heuh"). This time the post-positioned laughter marks her turn as non-serious and reinforces the tease, making it more explicit, and so does laughing at Lisa, which potentially disaffiliates with her and makes her the butt of a tease.

However, rather than accepting being the object of the tease, Lisa turns the situation around by laughing with the others at herself. She does this by adding a further quip (line 27: "as long hi hi as she's not hi got a crew cut hh hi"). It is noticeable that the turn is not only interspersed with laugher tokens but also upgrades the prior turn (from short to crew cut). In this way, Lisa transforms the tease from laughing at to laughing with, and so affiliates with the tease (Drew, 1987: 224). As Glenn (2003: 119) states: "willingness to go along with, or even initiate, laughter at oneself provides potential payoffs in realigning towards affiliation". Furthermore, this laughter is followed by collective laughter, so displaying the same stance, i.e. that Lisa's question was misplaced.

In short, we argue team spirit can be enacted in and through collective laughter. This collective laughter, in this case, is set up through a tease. The tease could be ignored (Drew, 1987), but in this case Lisa affiliates with the tease and transforms it from laughing at to laughing with, thus provoking collective laughter. Significantly, this enactment of affiliation and team spirit is at the expense of progressivity since the laughter has nothing directly to do with deciding whether Funky's fundraising activity should be included in the press or not. Ironically, and as discussed later, the doing of team spirit, at least through laughter, may militate against efficiency.

Extract 7.4: Impropriety and Team Spirit

At the end of the prior extract, there is a topic transition to another fundraising event and whether or not to include it in the press. This discussion is not included for reasons of space. In line 65, the topic returns to that of Funky.

Extract 7.4

65.	Amy	and why don't we ask him as well if we can still = because we
66.		don't know how much space they're giving you [do they Funky
67.	??	[yeah
68.		I'm going to do this next week and Funk = is it Funk or Funky
69.	Kira	Funky
70.	Dot	Funky
71.	Amy	Fun::ky
72.	Dot	they might do her next week
73.	Amy	Fu::nker
74.	Kira	she's not as Funky as her name sounds
75.	Amy	no I think I saw her she's quite like tiny isn't she ((Laughs))
76.		tiny wetty
77.		((collective laughter))

To gloss lines 65–68, Amy suggests asking him (i.e. the contact at the local press) if they can cover both the other event and Funky's event in the press the following week. In line 68, Amy initiates a repair ("is it Funk or Funky"). In the subsequent turns, Kira and Dot both provide the correct name. In line 71, Amy repeats Fu::nky, pronouncing it in a "funny" way by prolonging the vowel sound and stressing it. Dot, treating the question of whether it is Funk or Funky as an insertion sequence (i.e. a sequence of talk inserted between the first and second parts of an adjacency pair), provides a conditionally relevant response to Amy's initial suggestion that "they might do her next week". However, in the next turn, Amy disaligns with this and skip connects to her prior turn and continues transforming the name Funky—this time to Fu::nker—again pronouncing it in a funny way by stressing and prolonging the vowel sound. Kira orients this as an invitation to mock Funky and assesses her as "not being as Funky as her name sounds". She therefore displays an orientation to Funky as being in some way deviant because a singer called Funky should be Funky—which she is not. Not only does a first assessment make a second assessment a conditionally relevant next action but, as Pomerantz (1984) argues, there is a preference for agreement in which the second speaker affiliates with the first speaker. In this case, Amy aligns with this turn and affiliates, displaying that she shares the same stance. This is because her second assessment is upgraded, giving the first-hand grounds for her knowledge ("I saw her"), upgrading the negative assessment "not Funky" to tiny.

After this, she laughs, thus orienting the turn as humorous, and then upgrades her (negative) assessment of Funky from tiny to "tiny wetty". Jointly, therefore, Amy and Kira, through criticising a fundraiser, have performed an impropriety. As Jefferson et al. (1987: 160) note, by introducing improper talk (e.g. rudeness, crudeness, profanity, etc.), a speaker "may be offering an invitation to his [sic] co-participants to produce talk together whereby they can see themselves as intimate". In other words, if the invitation is accepted, together they will be constructing intimacy through affiliation (Jefferson et al., 1987). In this case, the co-constructed impropriety is affiliated with by collective laughter and so the group creates and displays an intimate relation based on their recognition of, and affiliation with, a move to relaxed, unguarded, spontaneous (i.e. intimate) interaction (Jefferson et al., 1987: 160).

Thus, as with the tease discussed in Extract 7.3, we see that Amy, through playing with the pronunciation of Funky, sets up a slot for criticising Funky. This results in a move to intimacy and affiliation which is cemented through collective laughter and so team spirit is potentially enacted. Similarly, as with Extract 7.3, this impropriety involves disalignment with the decision-making talk and a move into a play frame whereby actions, such as criticising a fundraiser, do not have the same moral consequences as they otherwise would (Holt, 2016). Counter-intuitively, then, one way of doing team spirit, as evidenced in group affiliation displayed in shared laughter, might be achieved in, and through, making inappropriate assessments which also impede the progression of the decision-making talk.

Extract 7.5: Self-Depreciation and Team Spirit

Once the collective laughter has died down, Amy self-selects to request that somebody who knows Funky could email her and set up the press release, after which they will set up a JustGiving page, i.e. a web page so that people can give to the charity. Following this, as discussed below, Amy self-teases, which promotes collective laughter and group affiliation, and so, we argue, potentially enacts team spirit.

Extract 7.5

Amy erm (.7) could you = could which one of you knows Funky (.) okay
so you email Funky and say we're not sure but if we could get
you <u>in</u> next week with a photo with all your hair (.) and then do

81.		JustGiving = sorry I can't help but od that can I↑
82.	Lisa	((Laughing)) every time
83.	Amy	((slight laugh)) no I'm sorry'cause I would never do that
84.		((laughter))

In line 80, Amy suggests that they do a "JustGiving" page, after which she latches on an apology for this action: "sorry I can't help but do that can I". Amy therefore apologises for wanting to set up a JustGiving page and accounts for it by saying she can't help herself, which is followed by a tag question (line 81: "can I↑") which projects agreement (Heritage, 2012: 14). Lisa orients the apology as ironic: setting up a JustGiving page is hardly an action that needs an apology from the head of fundraising. She displays this orientation by both laughing, which orients the prior turn as humorous, and by upgrading the frequency of the deviant behaviour (every time). Thus, she agrees, aligns, and affiliates with Amy's ironic aside. Amy then also laughs and continues the joke, apologising again because she would "never do that" (i.e. push for a JustGiving page to be set up). This continues the self-depreciating irony because she is in fact renowned for pushing to have JustGiving pages set up. Through laughing at herself, Amy invites the others to laugh with her rather than at her, which they do in the following turn. As Glenn (1991: 151) notes: "teasing oneself and inviting others to laugh at self represents one way to bring about shared laughter and this can prove useful for achieving affiliative displays".

Thus, again, in this short extract, Amy, through doing self-depreciating humour, sets up a slot which makes collective laughter relevant. The collective laughter displays that the group share the same stance, affiliate, and, as we argue, this is a potential way of doing team spirit. However, at the same time, we also note that laughter is achieved at the expense of progressivity towards deciding whether or not to include Funky in the press release.

Extract 7.6: Repair, Co-Authoring Utterances, and Teams

After the collective laughter has subsided, the team return to deciding how to deal with Funky's fundraising event.

Extract 7.6

85.	Dot	so come in this Friday (.) like on Friday
86.	Amy	no come in next Friday = no come in next Tuesday or Wednesday
87.	Lisa	ready for Friday
88.	Amy	to have a photo and (.) t-to have an article or whe-whether it's us
89.		or whether it's John to say why she's doing it and to have a
90.		just giving page set up
91.	Kira	she's got one set up
92.	Amy	she's got one set up okay
93.	Dot	we could do it next week and have before and after photographs
94.	Amy	and have this one (.) so in a way it'd be nice say next week
95.	Lisa	yeah
96.	Kira	yeah
97.	Amy	yeah if = if we can't (.2) and hear this coz it's important

In line 85, prefacing her turn with "so", Dot formulates the upshot of the talk so far, i.e. that Funky will come in this Friday. However, in line 86 Amy, without any dispreference markers such as hesitation or weak agreement, repairs: "no come in next Friday". In their seminal paper on repair, Schegloff et al. (1977) note that there is a preference for self-repair, yet in this case, other repair is achieved as a preferred action. Following Kangasharju (2002: 1452), the preference for other repair in institutional environments is accounted for by the fact that errors, such as confusing a date, may have a significant impact if not corrected and so the preference for self-repair is not oriented to in team talk. Thus, in team talk, the aligning but disaffiliating action of repairing is, counter-intuitively, a preferred and morally acceptable action. Amy then continues her turn, self-repairing (line 90: "no come in next Tuesday or Wednesday"). Lisa then adds an increment (line 87: "ready for Friday") to Amy's turn in progress which, as demonstrated in Extract 7.1, does being a team because the speakers co-author a turn and thus share the same stance. Amy then continues her turn, which ends by suggesting setting up a Just-Giving page. Kira then repairs this (line 91: "she's got one set up"). The preferred turn shape again displays a preference for other repair in team talk. Dot then suggests that they could do it next week and Amy adds an increment (line 94: "and have this one") and then gives the upshot of this suggestion: "so in a way it'd be nice say next week". Consequently, the turn is co-constructed, which means that the final decision is co-authored. In the following turns, Lisa and Kira also align with this and so a decision, in the shape of a commitment to future action, is announced and then accepted by the other team members. Once the decision to include Funky in the press is accepted, Amy changes topic to the importance of respecting the agreement that they have with the local press and making sure that the coverage of fundraising events in the local press is exclusive.

Discussions and Observations

As pointed out earlier in this chapter, team spirit may be something that is difficult to define but is something that people may have an intuitive grasp of and are able to recognise when they come across it. Using transcripts of naturally occurring meeting talk as data, and CA as a research methodology, this chapter has attempted to pinpoint in interactional terms when team spirit is enacted. To do this, we first argue that a team is not pre-discursive. Rather, teams are interactional accomplishments that are made visible in talk through actions such as co-authoring turns in progress (notably Extracts 7.1 and 7.6) and speaking as a team through, for example, the use of "we" (passim). Co-authoring turns in progress displays alignment and affiliation with the prior speaker and so is maximally pro-social, thus doing team spirit. While co-authored turns establish a potential for doing team spirit and for moving the decision-making talk forward, we also noted that there was much collective laughter in the interaction (notably Extracts 7.3, 7.4, and 7.5). Collective laughter displays a shared affective stance, does affiliation, and so also potentially establishes team spirit. Thus, establishing and sustaining a playful frame and laughter appears to be a significant element in promoting affiliation and promoting team spirit. Authors such as Katzenbach and Smith (2015) argue that fun and a sense of humour are essential to team performance, and management gurus such as Jack Welch even promoted the idea that work *should* be fun (Welch & Welch, 2015). However, if having fun, or at least laughing together, is an affiliative action that produces team spirit, how this is achieved interactionally is rarely the focus of such books.

Using CA as a research method, we show how joint laughter (and so affiliation and team spirit) is set up and enacted in talk. First, this is set up through teasing which, in this case, occurs when a team member asks a "stupid" question. By treating the question ironically, Amy invites laughing at Lisa. However, through recognising the tease and joining in with it by laughing with the others and extending the joke, Lisa transforms the laughing at to laughing with and so affiliation is achieved. Second, group laughter is achieved through doing an impropriety which involves criticising somebody who is setting up a charity event. This also leads to joint laughter and so becomes an opportunity to display affiliation and intimacy. Third, collective laughter is achieved through self-teasing which invites joint laughter and a display of affiliation. However, it is noticeable that this joint laugher does not come unexpectedly; rather, it is induced by Amy (the team leader) who sets up the tease by orienting Lisa's question as in some way misplaced and exaggerated (Extract 7.3), the impropriety by "playing" with the name (Extract 7.4), and the self-depreciation by doing an exaggerated and ironic apology for something that is laudable rather than blameworthy (Extract 7.5). Furthermore, we note that laughter, while initiated by Amy, does not depend on Amy alone; rather, it requires that other participants contribute to the shift to a play frame and so the group collectively arrives at joint laughter and affiliation.

However, it would be jumping to conclusions to argue that because joint laughter and the co-construction of turns that are affiliative necessarily enact team spirit. Rather, we argue that when such phenomena cluster across interactions, as they do in the decision-making episode of talk analysed in this chapter, they provide evidence of a more enduring phenomenon that could be described as team spirit. Of course, the threshold of deciding whether a cluster of affiliative actions is enough to establish team spirit remains a moot point. Nevertheless, we argue that for researchers and practitioners looking for team spirit, clusters of affiliative actions, as illustrated in this chapter, might be a good place to start. In this chapter, we have analysed one decision-making episode of talk which is replete with examples of affiliation which, we argue, enact team spirit. However, we also caution against assuming that the fundraising team *has* team spirit. Rather, we argue that team spirit is not something a team has, it is something they "do". Consequently, it is context-bound and in other instances, such as in arguments and disputes, it may be that the fundraising team is divided into two or more alliances, or interactional teams within a team, as, for example, Kangasharju (2002) and Gordon (2003) demonstrate, respectively, in the analyses of a meeting in a Finnish municipality and in family interaction.

Nevertheless, despite this drawback, we argue that the findings of this chapter can be useful to organisational scholars and that they can enable you to make visible, and thus analysable, something as apparently ephemeral as team spirit. Moreover, the findings of this chapter are based on direct observation of team spirit as it actually happens in real time.

They are neither reliant on surveys or questionnaires which give second-order accounts of how practitioners understand team spirit (cf. Silva et al., 2014), nor are they based on bland observations of management gurus, or post hoc recollections by practitioners. Through basing our analyses on direct observation and analysis of naturally occurring talk, we argue that the findings of this research could form the basis of advice to practitioners. Practitioners, especially team leaders, could be advised on how to achieve affiliation, i.e. through co-constructing turns at talk, promoting joint laughter, and referring to the team as an entity through the collective "we". However, this is not to say that the affiliative actions that are visible in this chapter are necessarily to be recommended as a way of doing team spirit in other situations. Corporate cultures no doubt vary from one organisation to the next so the way in which participants do affiliation in this case may not be acceptable in other organisations or even in other team configurations within the hospice. Indeed, the use of teasing, impropriety, and self-depreciation may be very high-risk strategies to adopt. And, at a national level, if we are to believe interculturalists, it could be argued that certain nationalities, such as the Germans, have a preference for being direct and frank and for disliking social chit-chat and banter of the type that we have seen in this chapter (Hall & Hall, 2000: 53).

Further, it is important to note that this chapter does not seek to comment on the effectiveness of the team analysed here. Indeed, it could be argued, as discussed before, that the play frame might not be efficient because it delays talk that is more relevant to the decision-making. And it could also be argued that (excessive) affiliation may lead to groupthink (Janis, 1982), whereby teams that are deeply cohesive and which strive for unanimity may not realistically appraise alternative courses of action and therefore may end up taking "bad" decisions. However, it is noticeable that, in the analyses presented in this chapter, while affiliation is omnipresent, there is also a preference for other repair so that erroneous claims are immediately corrected. More investigation would be required to establish if the doing of team spirit is conducive to groupthink or not.

Conclusions

In conclusion, we argue that CA as a method can make visible organisational phenomena such as team spirit that other methodologies may fail to reach. We note that most prior research into team spirit either used questionnaires to locate what team members considered team spirit to be or to measure the presence of team spirit, or at least an a priori definition of what the researcher considered team spirit to be. CA, on the other hand, through the use of transcripts of naturally occurring talk and its attention on the fine-grained details of sequences of talk, can make visible the doing of teams through such aspects of, to use Sacks' (1984) metaphor, the "machinery of talk", such as the co-authoring of turns, and the doing of laughter, improprieties, and teasing. Further, building on this, we argue that when clusters of affiliative actions occur, this may indicate that team spirit is being enacted. To come to this conclusion, we are, of course, using CA for non-CA purposes rather than following a more orthodox form of CA which would rely on the participants' own orientation to "team spirit". In other words, we are not focusing "just" on talk and the actions that it may be performing (such as affiliation); rather, we are drawing on an a priori common sense phenomenon (team spirit) that is considered to be an invisible ingredient of high-performing teams (Silva et al., 2014: 288). We are therefore treating CA as an analytical mentality and applying it to an issue of interest to organisational researchers. In doing so, we use CA to cross disciplinary boundaries and provide insights into how organisational phenomena are enacted as part of in situ practice. Further, we argue that once the machinery of talk with which teams and team spirit are enacted is made tangible, it can be offered to practitioners so that they may become more conscious of how teams function, and that this awareness may improve their practice.

In sum, if you adopt CA for your own research, you may be able to make phenomena of interest to you that may appear vague and slippery, tangible in talk, and observable as in situ practice. Using CA for non-CA purpose may therefore be a way of building bridges between researchers interested in the so-called "micro" sequential properties of talk and organisational scholars who are interested in how organisational phenomena, such as team spirit, are enacted as part of in situ social practice.

References

Abatecola, G., Mandarelli, G., & Poggesi, S. (2013). The personality factor: How top management teams make decisions—A literature review. *Journal of Management & Governance, 17*(4), 1073–1100.

Aboramadan, M. (2021). Top management teams characteristics and firms performance: Literature review and avenues for future research. *International Journal of Organizational Analysis, 29*(3), 603–628.

Antaki, C. (2011). Six kinds of applied conversation analysis. In C. Antaki (Ed.), *Applied conversation analysis: Intervention and change in institutional talk* (pp. 1–14). Palgrave.

Boden, D. (1994). *The business of talk: Organizations in action*. Polity Press.

Brounstein, M. (2009). *Managing teams for dummies*. Wiley.

Buttny, R. (2001). Therapeutic humor in retelling the clients' tellings. *Text, 21*(3), 303–326.

Clifton, J. (2014). Being in the know: Socio-epistemics and the communicative constitution of a management team. *Organization Management Journal, 11*, 1–11.

Clifton, J., & Rømer Barfod, J. (forthcoming). Conversation analysis in qualitative organizational communication research. In B. Brummans, B. Taylor, & A. Sivunen (Eds.), *The Sage handbook of qualitative research in organizational communication*. Sage.

Cohen, S. G., & Bailey, D. E. (1997). What makes teams work: Group effectiveness research from the shop floor to the executive suite. *Journal of management, 23*(3), 239–290.

Costa, A. C. (2003). Work team trust and effectiveness. *Personnel Review, 32*(5), 605–622.

Day, D., Gronn, P., & Salas, E. (2004). Leadership capacity in teams. *The Leadership Quarterly, 15*(6), 857–880.

Deppermann, A. (2013). Multimodal interaction from a conversation analytic perspective. *Journal of Pragmatics, 46*(1), 1–7.

Djordjilovic, O. (2012). Displaying and developing team identity in workplace meetings—A multimodal perspective. *Discourse Studies, 14*, 111–127.

Drew, P. (1987). Po-faced receipts of teases. *Linguistics, 25*(1), 219–253.

Drew, P. (2005). Conversation analysis. In K. Fitch & R. Sanders (Eds.), *Handbook of language and social interaction* (pp. 71–102). Lawrence Erlbaum.

Ford, C. (2012). Clarity in applied and interdisciplinary conversation analysis. *Discourse Studies, 14*(4), 507–513.

Ford, C., Fox, B., & Thompson, S. (2002). Constituency and the grammar of turn increments. In C. Ford, B. Fox, & S. Thompson (Eds.), *The language of turn and sequence* (pp. 14–38). Oxford University Press.

Glenn, P. (1991). Current speaker initiation of two-party shared laughter. *Research on Language & Social Interaction, 25*(1–4), 139–162.

Glenn, P. (2003). *Laughter in interaction*. Cambridge University Press.

Gordon, C. (2003). Aligning as a team: Forms of conjoined participation in (stepfamily)interaction. *Research on Language and Social Interaction, 36*(4), 395–431.

Hall, E., & Hall, M. (2000). *Understanding cultural differences: Germans*. Intercultural Press.

Hamilton, P. (2021). *Supercharged teams: Power your team with the tools for success*. Pearson.

Heerman, B. (2003). Team spirit: Deepening team awareness of service to customers. *The Journal for Quality and Participation, 26*(4), 40–43.

Heritage, J. (2012). Epistemics in action: Action formation and territories of knowledge. *Research on Language & Social Interaction, 45*(1), 1–29.

Hertel, G., Geister, S., & Konradt, U. (2005). Managing virtual teams: A review of current empirical research. *Human Resource Management Review, 15*(1), 69–95.

Holt, E. (2016). Laughter at last: Playfulness and laughter in interaction. *Journal of Pragmatics, 100*, 89–102.

Housley, W. (2000). Story, narrative and teamwork. *The Sociological Review, 48*(3), 425–443.

Huisman, M. (2001). Decision-making in meetings as talk-in-interaction. *International Studies of Management & Organization, 31*(3), 69–90.

Hutchby, I., & Wooffitt, R. (2008). *Conversation analysis*. Polity.

Janis, I. (1982). *Groupthink*. Haughton Mifflin.

Jaworski, B. J., & Kohli, A. K. (1993). Market orientation: Antecedents and consequences. *Journal of Marketing, 57*(3), 53–70.

Jefferson, G., Sacks, H., & Schegloff, E. (1987). Notes on laughter in the pursuit of intimacy. In G. Button & J. Lee (Eds.), *Talk and social organization* (pp. 152–205). Multilingual Matters.

Kangasharju, H. (1996). Aligning as a team in multiparty conversation. *Journal of Pragmatics, 26*, 291–319.

Kangasharju, H. (2002). Alignment in disagreement: Forming oppositional alliances in committee meetings. *Journal of Pragmatics, 34*(10–11), 1447–1471.

Katzenbach, J., & Smith, D. (2015). *The wisdom of teams: Creating the high-performance organization*. Harvard Business Review Press.

Kozlowski, S. W. J., & Bell, B. S. (2003). Work groups and teams in organizations. In W. C. Borman, D. R. Ilgen, & R. J. Klimoski (Eds.), *Handbook of psychology (Vol. 12): Industrial and organizational psychology* (pp. 333–375). Wiley-Blackwell.

Lee, S. H., & Tanaka, H. (2016). Affiliation and alignment in responding actions. *Journal of Pragmatics, 100*, 1–7.

Lerner, G. (1993). Collectivities in action: Establishing the relevance of conjoined participation in conversation. *Text, 13*(2), 213–245.
Levi, D. (2015). *Group dynamics for teams*. Sage.
Lindström, A., & Sorjonen, M.-L. (2013). Affiliation in conversation. In J. Sidnell & T. Stivers (Eds.), *The handbook of conversation analysis* (pp. 350–370). Wiley Blackwell.
Marakaki, V., Merlino, S., Mondada, L., & Oloff, F. (2010). Laughter in professional meetings: The organization of an emergent ethnic joke. *Journal of Pragmatics, 42*, 1526–1542.
Nielsen, M. F. (2009). Interpretative management in business meetings: Understanding managers' interactional strategies through conversation analysis. *The Journal of Business Communication, 46*(1), 23–56.
Oittinen, T. (2018). Multimodal accomplishment of alignment and affiliation in the local space of distant meetings. *Culture and Organization, 24*(1), 31–53.
Pentland, A. (2012). The new science of building great teams. *Harvard Business Review, 90*(4), 60–70.
Peräkylä, A. (2011). Validity in research on naturally occurring social interaction. In D. Silverman (Ed.), *Qualitative research* (pp. 365–382). Sage.
Pomerantz, A. (1984). Agreeing and disagreeing with assessments: Some features of preferred/dispreferred turn shapes. In J. M. Atkinson & J. Heritage (Eds.), *Structures of social action* (pp. 57–101). Cambridge University Press.
Rabha, M. (no date). *5 ways to encourage team spirit*. https://blog.vantagecircle.com/team-spirit/
Ratzmann, M., Pesch, R., Bouncken, R., & Climent, C. M. (2018). The price of team spirit for sense-making through task discourse in innovation teams. *Group Decision and Negotiation, 27*(3), 321–341.
Sacks, H. (1984). Notes on methodology. In J. M. Atkinson & J. Heritage (Eds.), *Structures of social action* (pp. 21–27). Cambridge University Press.
Sacks, H. (1992). *Lectures on conversation* (2 vols, edited by Gail Jefferson with introduction by Emanuel A. Schegloff). Blackwell.
Sacks, H., Schegloff, E. A., & Jefferson, G. (1974). A simplest systematics for the organization of turn taking for conversation. *Language, 50*(4), 696–735.
Salojärvi, H., & Saarenketo, S. (2013). The effect of teams on customer knowledge processing, esprit de corps and account performance in international key account management. *European Journal of Marketing, 47*(5/6), 987–1005.
Schegloff, E. (1995). Parties and talking together: Two ways in which numbers are significant for talk-in-interaction. In P. ten Have & G. Psathas (Eds.), *Situated order: Studies in the social organization of talk and embodied* (pp. 31–42). University Press of America.
Schegloff, E. A., Jefferson, G., & Sacks, H. (1977). The preference for self-correction in the organization of repair in conversation. *Language, 53*(2), 361–382.

Seedhouse, P. (2005). Conversation analysis and language learning. *Language Teaching, 38*(4), 165–187.
Sidnell, J., & Stivers, T. (Eds.). (2013). *The handbook of conversation analysis*. Wiley-Blackwell.
Silva, T., Cunha, M. P. E., Clegg, S. R., Neves, P., Rego, A., & Rodrigues, R. A. (2014). Smells like team spirit: Opening a paradoxical black box. *Human Relations, 67*(3), 287–310.
Sinclair, A. (1992). The tyranny of a team ideology. *Organization Studies, 13*(4), 611–626.
Stivers, T., Mondada, L., & Steensig, J. (2011). Knowledge, morality and affiliation in social interaction. In T. Stivers, L. Mondada, & J. Steensig (Eds.), *The morality of knowledge in conversation* (pp. 3–26). Cambridge University Press.
Svennevig, J. (2012). Interaction in workplace meetings. *Discourse Studies, 14*(1), 3–10.
ten Have, P. (2007). *Doing conversation analysis*. Sage.
Welch, J., & Welch, S. (2015). *The real-life MBA*. Harper Collins.

CHAPTER 8

Ventriloquism and the Importance of the Other-Than-Human in Organisational Interaction

Introduction

To do is causing to do (Latour, 1996). This observation lays the basis for the Montreal School's approach to interaction which, in a nutshell, focuses not only on the actions that are performed through talk but also on what causes these actions. This is achieved by drawing on a ventriloquial metaphor whereby, in much the same way as the ventriloquist makes a dummy speak, organisational players implicitly or explicitly draw on "things that matter" in their talk and attribute the genesis of their actions and words to these, and reflexively these "things that matter" make the organisational player speak and do things. As Latour (2010: xiv) makes clear, "if it is possible 'to do things with words' it is even truer that many *things* make us do words" (italics in original). Thus, unlike the other chapters in this book, in this chapter we focus not only on human interaction but also on what motivates such language use, and we take a sociomaterial approach to the analysis of naturally occurring interaction.

More specifically, using transcripts of a naturally occurring talk between Amy and Kit in which Kit presents a problem to her hierarchic superior (Amy), we demonstrate how other-than-human entities (i.e. "things that matter") such as organisational protocols, insurance policies, and events become relevant to the interaction. This is because these "things that matter" are attributed agency and so cause organisational players to do

E. Darics and J. Clifton, *Organisation, Communication and Language*, New Perspectives in Organizational Communication,
https://doi.org/10.1007/978-3-031-30199-5_8

things. Therefore, instead of taking an anthropocentric view of the world in which humans determine and control the material world, a ventriloquial approach considers that humans not only enact the material world but also react to it. This is because this material world causes them to do things.

This chapter is structured as follows. First, we provide an overview of the Montreal School's sociomaterial approach to analysis. Second, we present an example of a ventriloquial analysis and focus on the way in which authority and accountability are enacted by a network of both human and other-than-human agents. Third, we draw out what a ventriloquial analysis can add to the discursive analyses of talk at work that have been provided in the previous chapters.

The Montreal School

The Montreal School is the name sometimes given to an approach to analysis mainly associated with François Cooren, Professor of Communication at the University of Montreal, and colleagues. While, as McPhee and Iveson (2013) point out, it is perhaps dangerous to assume a uniformity among the various researchers who may identify with this school, nevertheless, there are certain key assumptions that form the core of the Montreal School's approach to analysing communication. First and foremost, as mentioned previously, is the notion of ventriloquism, which Cooren (2015: 476) defines as: "actions through which someone or something makes someone or something say or do things". This is a metaphor that seeks to capture the essence of communication by likening it to the way in which vents (the technical term for a ventriloquist) make their figures (the technical term for the ventriloquist's dummy) speak. If we take such a metaphor seriously, this allows us to analyse not only what is said or done but also to investigate what causes these actions to be done and words to be said. Further, ventriloquism also implies that it is not only the vent who makes figures speak and act. The figures also cause the vent to speak and do things. This gives rise to a refinement of the ventriloquial metaphor and divides it into two notions: upstream and downstream ventriloquism. Upstream ventriloquism refers to the flow of agencies that make humans (and other actants) do things and speak. Downstream ventriloquism refers to the way in which humans (and other actants) make other agencies speak and act. These two forms of ventriloquism are part of the ventriloquial metaphor which aids understanding and analysis. They are not to be understood as distinct either/or entities. Rather, because there is a continuous oscillation between the two forms of agency, they are reflexive, intertwined, and indivisible (Caronia & Cooren, 2014).

Cooren and Matté (2010) exemplify ventriloquism in action in their analysis of President Obama's swearing in ceremony in which Obama repeats an oath, originally authored by George Washington, after the Chief Justice. Cooren and Matté (2010) argue that such an interaction can be more fully understood by moving beyond the limits of purely human interaction between the swearer of the oath (Obama) and the administrator of the oath (the Chief Justice). They (Cooren & Matté, 2010) argue that the interaction can be better understood if you take into account figures such as the American Constitution, which was invoked by both parties to talk. In this way, the Constitution can be said to have been ventriloquised and animated by the Chief Justice and Obama (downstream ventriloquism), and, reflexively, the American Constitution can be said to have animated and caused Obama and the Chief Justice to say and do the things they said and did (upstream ventriloquism). To ignore this ventriloquial effect is to ignore an essential aspect of the interaction and to overlook what made a swearing in ceremony *the* swearing in ceremony in which the constitution of the USA makes a difference. Of course, it could be argued that the constitution has no agency and is simply manipulated by the human actors. This would be consistent with a Goffmanian analysis of the principal, author, and animator whereby the principle is the *person* responsible for the message, the author is the *person* responsible for the form of the utterance, and the animator is the *person* who actually utters the words (Goffman, 1981). However, Cooren and Matté (2010) argue that attributing agency to the text (i.e. the oath as it is sworn and written by the founding fathers of the USA) is to recognise the activity of the delegation of agency that the founding fathers of the USA enshrined in the text and which can be transported across space and time and made relevant in other situations. The text animates the Chief Justice and Obama, and Obama and the Chief Justice are animated by the text, which makes it present and consequential to the interaction. If we deny such agency to the text, this is tantamount to denying the difference it makes in a given situation. This is because, as Cooren and Matté (2010: 17) write:

> the constitution of any institutional or social event results from the activity of various forms of agencies that participate in its performance or actualization. As analysts, we should not leave the realm of practice, action and doings, but we then need to acknowledge all the beings or (what we propose to call) figures that appear to make a difference, i.e., do something, in a given situation.

This key notion of ventriloquism, therefore, traces its roots back to actor network theory (ANT) (Callon, 1986; Latour, 2005). Central to an understanding of ANT is the idea of generalised symmetry which advocates that non-human entities such as artefacts, ideas, processes, texts, and so on are as important as humans in creating the social world. Consequently, when we seek to explain sociological phenomena, we should consider equally the agency of both human and non-human actants. Cooren et al. (2012) exemplify how this works through their discussion of the National Rifle Association's (NRA) slogan: "Guns don't kill. People kill people". Such a slogan assumes the primacy of human action. However, without the gun the human could not shoot someone to death.

Consequently, there is necessarily an interplay between the material and the human. From an ANT perspective, this interplay is explained through the notion that when an agent (whether human or not) acts, they are in fact the visible face of a network of a plenum of agencies. In the case of the NRA's slogan, the agent is not only the human who pulls the trigger. Rather, agency consists of a network of other agencies such as material artefacts (the gun), the second amendment to the US constitution that allows American citizens to bear arms, the historical reasoning behind the amendment that led to the right to bear arms, the NRA and its supporters who advocate the right to bear arms, and so on. The upshot of this is that agency is always hybrid and should always be considered to be shared across a plenum of intertwined agencies, both human and non-human, that cause somebody or something to act (Latour, 1996).

This plenum of agencies consists therefore of the human and the material. Materiality in this sense is understood not only in terms of physical objects (such as the gun) but also in terms of "things that matter" (such as the second amendment) which act on somebody or something. This is because, as Cooren et al. (2012: 301) argue, the etymological roots of the word "matter" come from the Latin word *materia*, which means both "the substance from which something is made" and the "grounds, reason or cause for something". Thus, materiality, from a ventriloquial perspective, not only refers to physical objects but also to what causes something, as in the expression "what's the matter?", meaning what is the cause of a particular state of mind or behaviour. As Cooren et al. (2012: 301) put it: "materiality relates to what is relevant or pertinent to a given situation". These "things that matter" may therefore be literally anything ranging from values, beliefs, policies, ideologies, passions, situations, organisations, other people, and so on—*provided that* they are "granted to be the source of action" (Latour, 1996: 373).

In the example of the NRA's slogan, there is nothing that links the notion of actor networks with interaction. This link was provided by the Montreal School who, as Fairhurst and Cooren (2009: 474) put it, gave ANT an "interactional and organizational twist". This interactional twist to ANT relies on the fine-grained analysis of transcripts of naturally occurring interaction so that, in Cooren's terms, ventriloquial analyses never leave the terra firma of interaction (Cooren, 2012: 8). Using transcripts of naturally occurring talk as data allows the analyst to identify, on the one hand, the figures that are implicitly or explicitly invoked by the participants themselves and which are animated by people. And, on the other hand, never leaving the terra firma of interaction allows us to identify the vents that are implicitly or explicitly invoked and which animate figures, and vice versa (Nathues et al., 2021). Such fine-grained analyses rely to some extent on the terminology of conversation analysis (see Chapter 7) and a rigorous analysis of sequences of talk that demonstrates the participants' orientation to these figures and their consequentiality to the interaction. However, in stark contrast to CA, a ventriloquial analysis does not shy away from demonstrating the procedural consequentiality of "things that matter". This is not to say that "anything goes" and that we can foist our concerns willy-nilly on the participants. If you adopt a ventriloquial approach to analysis, you must still demonstrate that the participants are orienting to a particular network of actants and that this network is consequential to the interaction.

Such an approach to interaction is therefore considerably different to the discursive approaches showcased in this book so far that treat interaction as a purely human affair in which atomised humans communicate with each other. Such an anthropocentric approach to interaction is, as Castor and Cooren (2006: 573) argue, insufficient to capture a fully nuanced account of what is going on because it "tends to leave aside other entities that appear to compose and structure this world—machines, documents, organisations, policies, architectural elements, signs, and procedures, to just name a few". Conversely, it is argued that a ventriloquial approach allows us to make visible, and thus analysable, the way in which other entities ("things that matter") cause humans to act. In short, it is argued that we should consider not only what people are doing in an interaction but also "what leads them to do what they are doing, that is, what animates them in a specific situation or in their daily activities, as well as what speaks or acts through them, that is, what constitutes them and what they constitute as social or organizational agents" (Cooren et al., 2012: 297). In this way, the Montreal School adopts a stance that cancels the divide between the material and the discursive worlds and, taking the notion of generalised symmetry seriously, considers the social and the material as an ensemble rather than as discrete and separate entities.

The Data

The data for this chapter come from a meeting between Amy and Kit. In the extracts analysed below, Kit recounts some issues that she had during a recent fundraising activity. The problem is that the crowd at the festival had been rowdy and violent towards the fundraisers who were wearing Minion[1] costumes. Despite this, Gabby, Sarah, and some other volunteer fundraisers had allowed children to wear the Minion costumes. Kit had requested "a hundred times" that the children take off the costumes, but they had ignored her. The narrative account of these events takes the form of a problem in search of a solution. The solution to the problem is provided by Amy who suggests introducing a policy and who, in a hypothetical narrative of future events, stories the imagined future events to demonstrate that having a policy statement will solve the issue. Through operationalising the Montreal School's key metaphor of ventriloquism, we show how the interplay between various agents—human, textual, and other-than-human—allows the organisational players to (1) enact, albeit in an imagined scenario, authority through ventriloquising the hospice's policies, and (2) account for their actions and justify decisions.

[1] Minions are fantasy characters in a popular computer-animated film franchise.

Doing Ventriloquial Analyses

The Montreal School is more of a loose collection of scholars who share similar research interests than a monolithic approach to investigation. Consequently, as Nathues et al. (2021) remark, there is no single methodological framework that provides guidance for researchers wishing to either show how a person is led to say what he/she says or does what he/she does, or what voices can be recognised in what he/she is saying or doing. Ventriloquial analyses have thus drawn on various methods of analysis data such as interviews (Wilhoit & Kisselburgh, 2019), narrative (Cooren, 2001), ethnography (Bencherki, 2016), and fine-grained analyses of short extracts of transcriptions of naturally occurring talk in the CA tradition (Clifton & de la Broise, 2020), the latter perhaps being, as Bencherki (2014: 147, our translation) puts it, "the method privileged by the Montreal School".

In this chapter, we draw on two traditions: narrative and CA. The data are in the form of a future hypothetical story which we analyse in terms of the social practice of storytelling (see Chapter 5). However, unlike Chapter 5, we carry out the analyses using the jargon of CA, but unlike CA (see Chapter 7), we take into account the extra-local networks of actants, whether human or other-than-human, which the participants use to account for their actions.

First, then, as with any fine-grained analysis of naturally occurring talk, an excerpt must be selected. In this case, this particular excerpt was selected because at first glance, it appeared to illustrate the importance of protocols and texts (i.e. the other-than-human) to the communicative constitution of the organisation. The data was transcribed, and it was at this point that the narrative form of the interaction became clear and we adopted a CA-inspired narrative as a social practice approach to analysis. However, key to an analysis from a ventriloquial perspective is identifying the vents (the speakers) and figures (what is animating the speakers), whether human or other-than-human, that are invoked or come to express themselves in the interaction and which make a difference to that interaction. Focusing on the vents and the network of actors (human or other-than-human) that *the participants make observably relevant* to the interaction allows us to scale up, i.e. to investigate, how the local talk produces the extra-local, the organisation writ large. In other words, it allows us to look beyond the talk to gain an understanding of what acts on the participant beyond the local talk and what leads them to talk as they talk, or act as they act. It is through scaling up that ventriloquial analyses can combine fine-grained analyses of talk with phenomena of interest to organisational scholars, such as "authority", and show how they are brought off as members' accomplishments in the here and now of localised interaction.

The Analyses

Extract 8.1: The Problem

At the beginning of the extract, Kit, one of the fundraisers, discusses a recent fundraising event which involved the fundraisers dressing up in Minion outfits. In the talk immediately prior to this extract, Kit explained some of the problems they had had, notably with the appropriateness of the T-shirts they had been wearing and the fact that the public had been rowdy.

Extract 8.1

1	Kit	umm so that was one of the feedback that I got umm the minion
2		costumes while they kind of worked ((sighs))
3	Amy	frightening↑
4	Kit	it was (.) it well I found it okay because I got rugby tackled a
5		couple times but people just forgetting
6	Amy	.hhhh
7	Kit	we were in costumes PUNCHED a couple of times
8	Amy	did you
9	Kit	and got head-butted, people were a bit violent [but then
10	Amy	[((laughs)) OKAY
11	Kit	when we got out of the minion costumes = got out of the minion costumes
12		and went and did sales I got back and Gabby had put children in
13	Kit	the minion costumes ((laughs)) to which I was like no::::
14		get them out [((laughs))
15	Amy	[okay okay
16	Kit	umm and that happened a few times I locked it in the van
17	Amy	okay
18	Kit	and then when I went out Sarah was=they got them out of the van
19		and put (.) it was her son and I think one of the other volunteer's kids
20		it wasn't (.) members of the public but still it wasn't okay and they just

21		did not listen a hundred times I said no get the kids out of the costumes
22	Amy	okay
23	Kit	but it was difficult

In line 1, Kit closes down the prior topic—the first piece of feedback she received about the fundraising event—and shifts topic to the next piece of feedback: the Minion costumes. The upcoming problem is recounted in a narrative form. First, Kit states that the Minion costumes "kind of worked" and then closes her turn with a deep sigh. This orients the recipient to the upcoming problematic nature of the feedback. Amy responds to this negative assessment with an upgraded assessment (i.e. upgrading from "kind of worked" to "frightening"). The upgrade is spoken with a rising intonation, thus marking it as a candidate description requiring confirmation in the next turn. However, Kit disaligns with this upgrade and downgrades her assessment of the events by saying "it was okay". She then accounts for this assessment on the grounds that she got rugby tackled a couple of times (line 4), punched (line 7), and headbutted (line 9), summing it up with the downgraded assessment "people were a bit violent" (line 7).

After having topicalised, but downgraded, the violent consequences of wearing the costumes, Kit (line 11) introduces the complicating action (i.e. the core of the story, which sets up a situation that has to be resolved). In this case, the complicating action is that after the fundraisers, including Kit, had taken off the Minion costumes and while they were doing sales, "Gabby had put CHILDREN in the Minion costumes". This is followed by laughter which, as Shaw et al. (2013) demonstrate, provides a way of softening or neutralising the turn so that it negates the need for an immediate recipient response that might hinder the progress of the talk. In this case, Amy does not seek to take a turn and Kit, switching to reconstructed dialogue, recounts the story as a dialogue which engages and involves the recipient in a more vivid portrayal of events (Tannen, 1989). Kit reconstructs what she said to Gabby: "I was like no::: get them out" (lines 13–14). She then continues her turn to add that this happened a few times, thus stressing that it was a persistent and wilful act of disobedience. In order to resolve the complicating action, Kit locked the costumes in the van (line 16). However, this solution is revealed to be insufficient. In lines 18 ff., Kit continues the story: when she was away,

Sarah got the costumes out of the van and put them on the kids, her son, and one of the other volunteer's kids (lines 18–19). Even though it was not members of the public who were wearing the costumes, Kit still evaluates the action negatively (line 20: "but still it wasn't okay"). The repetitive nature of this problem is then emphasised again and, shifting once more to a reconstructed dialogue, Kit states that even though she said a hundred times "no, get the kids out of the costumes", they "just did not listen". In line 22, Amy acknowledges receipt of the story ("okay") and Kit adds a turn to evaluate the situation as "difficult" (line 23: "but it was difficult").

In sum, in Extract 8.1 Kit sets out a problem that is in search of a solution. It is in the authoring of the solution for the problem that both Kit and Amy animate other-than-human agents as "things that matter" either to provide a solution to the problem and/or to account for the problem/solution.

Extract 8.2: The Solution

Having set out the problem, it now becomes incumbent on the line manager (Amy) to find a solution.

Extract 8.2

1	Amy	so (.) that probably leads (.) me to add onto the list then, when we do the
2		minions paper (.) what we're gonna do with them we need a little policy
3		[that(.) so that you can also be saying this is the policy↑
4	Kit	[yeah
5	Kit	yeah
6	Amy	as opposed to I'm Kit telling you all what to do you know and I'm (.)
7		your ( ) you know I'm sure that wasn't a particularly comfortable place to be
8	Kit	no ((laughs)) it's just they're no = they're not insured [if they get hurt
9	Amy	[yeah okay
10	Kit	it was so hot in the costume [some of the time. [once they're doing
11	Amy	[yeah [yeah
12	Amy	yeah
13	Kit	and because there were drunks wandering around they just
14	Amy	no no I hear you ((laughs))
15	Kit	it was sort of terrifying ((laughs)) it's like oh God please don't do that
16	Amy	I suppose what we can do is (0.5) and I s'pose we have to have this question

17		are we gonna rent them out↑ and therefore if they wanted to rent them
18		and own them that would be their problem [but not = not on our watch
19	Kit	[yeah
20		sort of thing
21	Kit	yeah
22	Amy	yeah okay do you think it did as well as flowers at ((name of festival))

In lines 24 ff., Amy gives the solution to the problem: "so (.) that probably leads (.) me to add onto the list then when we do the minions paper (.) what we're gonna do with them, we need a little policy [that (.) so that you can also be saying this is the policy". The deictic marker "that" (line 24: "that probably leads me") refers back to the events. Consequently, she orients the events as being agentive in leading her to offer her solution to the problem, i.e. drawing up a little policy. As Cooren (2010: 7, italics in original) notes: "our actions seem meaningful or accountable because we appear to be (or present ourselves as) *moved* by specific reasons that *authorize*, *allow*, or *lead* us to do what we do whether these reasons are institutional, ethical, practical, [or] ideological". Thus, in this case, Amy (downstream) ventriloquises these events, so presentifying them (i.e. "making present things and beings that, although not physically present, can influence the unfolding of a situation" [Benoit-Barné & Cooren, 2009: 10]) in the here and now of the interaction. Moreover, she attributes agency to them since they are leading her to suggest a particular solution to the problem of the unauthorised use of the Minion costumes. Further, attributing agency to these events also renders the suggestion to have a little policy accountable in the ethnomethodological sense of justifying, explaining, or making an action intelligible on demand (Garfinkel, 1967).

After having suggested they need a little policy, Amy imagines a future situation in which Kit "can also be saying this is the policy". Kit aligns with this suggestion as it is in progress (line 49: "yeah") and at the end of Amy's turn (line 50: "yeah"). In the continuation of her suggestion, Amy contrasts this imagined future situation with the past situation in which Kit was only able to say: "I'm Kit telling you all what to do, you know, and I'm (.) your ()". Amy then assesses this past situation as something that "wasn't a particularly comfortable place to be", with which Kit aligns (line 46: "no").

The little policy is therefore set up in a future imagined scenario so that Kit can justify her action of telling the volunteers to stop allowing the children to use the costumes and so be in a more comfortable situation. This is because, as Benoit-Barné and Cooren (2009) argue, the policy will "do" authority and will authorise her to tell the children to stop wearing the costumes. Authority has been defined by Weber (1978) as having three pure types: traditional, charismatic, and rational-legal. Rational-legal authority is defined as "a belief in the legality of patterns of normative rules and the right of those elevated to authority under such rules to issue commands" (Weber, 1978: 215). Essential to the notion of authority is that one gives up one's own private judgement in deference to somebody who, or something that, is oriented to as having authority. In this case, Amy projects that the volunteers' private judgement of allowing the kids to wear the costumes will be surrendered to Kit's future imagined utterance "this is the policy". This utterance, in the imagined scenario at least, will enact rational-legal authority because, on the one hand, the policy invokes a normative rule (what should be done) and, on the other hand, because Kit has the right to issue such an instruction. Thus, the policy is imagined to be an agent that makes the difference in the future hypothetical situation. Without the policy Kit has no authority, and, as past events have revealed, the volunteers will not surrender their private judgement.

In the future imagined scenario, authority will be enacted by Kit (downstream) ventriloquising the policy. Through invoking the policy, she will be able to speak on behalf of the charity, and so the organisation also co-authors her interdiction to wear the Minion costumes. It is not "just Kit" speaking; rather, it is the hybrid presence of both Kit and the organisation which is co-authoring her words. As Cooren (2010: 113) states, "being the author of what is put forward presupposes that we be or appear authorized, which precisely means that we share authorship with what or who authorizes us to say what we say". In this case, the who or what that authorises Kit to say "this is policy" is the organisation that wrote the policy. Significantly, it is noted that "just being Kit" and "telling you all what to do" is not enough to get the others to surrender their private judgement. As Bourgoin and Bencherki (2013: 12) note, authority is:

> presenting oneself as being moved or animated by those other entities and sharing one's authorship with them. I share my authorship of the action with the cause I invoke, and in a sense it is also my own position as an

actor that is authored by that cause. For each action to be authoritative, therefore, one needs to distribute its authorship among other agents.

Further, if the policy is written, it will contribute to stabilising the organisation. This is because it will have a degree of permanence that spoken words do not, and as a text it can be transported across time and space (as previously noted in the discussion concerning Obama's swearing in ceremony and the American Constitution). The text, therefore, becomes an artefact that is potentially relevant and consequential to any future interaction and so as an organisational text it stabilises, albeit for a fleeting moment, the emergence of the organisation, to borrow a term from Garfinkel (1967), for another first time. It is in this way that organisations are said to be communicatively constituted. And, as Cooren (2012: 6) notes, "if there is anything that we call an organisation, a society, or even a country, it must exist through all these ventriloquial effects/incarnations/materializations/reifications" that communicate it into being.

In the next turn, Kit aligns with Amy's assessment that trying to convince people to surrender their judgement and that allowing the kids to wear the costumes "wasn't a particularly comfortable place to be". Kit then accounts for her attempt to stop them wearing the costumes: "It's just, they're no = they're not insured if they get hurt". Her action is thus justified, explained, and accounted for by ventriloquising what led her to attempt to stop the children wearing the costumes (i.e. the fact that they were not insured). The lack of a "thing that matters" (i.e. the insurance) is attributed to agency in causing her to take a particular course of action. Thus, as with the policy that Amy suggests, another document can be seen to be constitutive of the organisation and can be ventriloquised to account for particular actions. Through accounting for a particular action by ventriloquising the insurance (policy), the organisation is therefore once again invoked and communicatively constituted as one that, as with most organisations, has insurance policies. Moreover, these insurance policies are agentive in constraining and allowing certain actions which thus constitute the organisation in a particular way. In short, the organisation is constituted not only in and through human interaction but also in and through the agents that Kit mobilises to account for her actions.

In the continuation of her turn, Kit continues to account for her attempt to stop the others wearing the costumes (line 33, "because it was so hot in the costume", and line 36, "because there were drunks wandering around"). She assesses these events as "sort of terrifying" and this causes her to say to herself: "oh God please don't do that". Thus, she accounts for her actions and renders them explainable and justifiable on the grounds that she was led to take such action because of external events (i.e. the heat and the drunks), as well as the lack of insurance as previously discussed. In short, the heat and the drunks caused her to act. Thus, in the network of "things that matter" that cause her to act are other humans (the drunks) and the weather.

This account and assessment of the situation as a problem (line 38: "it was sort of terrifying") leads to another suggestion to solve the problem. In line 39, Amy suggests that "we could rent them [i.e. the costumes] out". In this case, the problem is not necessarily solved but is no longer the organisation's problem. Any possible violence and hurt related to wearing the costumes becomes the renter's problem and doesn't happen on our watch (line 41). Kit aligns with this suggestion (lines 42 and 44: "yeah") and then Amy closes down the topic of the Minion costumes ("yeah okay") and shifts topic to whether Kit thinks it "did as well as flowers at (name of festival)" (line 45).

Observations for Research

As Carlile et al. (2013: 2) have suggested, despite the fact that the linguistic turn has been hiding the material from view, there is now an increasing move to bring materiality back into organisational studies and to investigate the ways in which materiality matters in organisational activity. The Montreal School is at the forefront of such a movement and seeks to consider how "things that matter" are ventriloquised, animated, and made consequential to the organisation (downstream ventriloquism) and, reflexively, how things that matter animate organisational players (upstream ventriloquism) and so make a difference to the organisation as it is communicatively constituted.

If we scale up from the micro-interactions and locate the networks of actants that are made relevant and consequential to the here and now of interaction, we can make visible, and therefore analysable, the way in which the organisation and its landscape speaks through the utterances of organisational players, and, reflexively, how organisational players make the organisation and its landscape speak, and so communicatively constitute it (Cooren et al., 2011). This proposition therefore adds to purely discursive work on the enactment of organisation by pointing to the importance of not only the human but also other "things that matter" in the communicative constitution of organisation. By so doing, ventriloquism calls into question the prevalent reduction of communication to people interacting with one another and shows that interactions include additional elements of a situation that are voiced through what people say or do. As such, the notion of ventriloquism significantly nuances anthropocentric approaches to organisation that often overlook the material. In the ANT tradition, from a ventriloquial perspective, human actants are considered to be spokespeople for networks made up of a plenum of agencies that are speaking through the human. The argument is that in situ workplace practice—organising—is always generated through networks of human and non-human agents, or as Law (1992: 384) states: "an actor is also, always, a network". It is this network and its agentivity that a ventriloquial approach to communication encourages the researcher to consider.

More specifically, in this chapter we have demonstrated (1) how authority is enacted in a future hypothetical narrative of dealing with a problem, and (2) how actions in the *here and now* are accounted for in and through ventriloquism. First, we note that, in Amy's future story, authority is not enacted by Kit acting as "just" Kit, an atomised human. Rather, it is enacted by Kit ventriloquising a policy which presentifies "the organisation" and which co-authors her instruction not to wear the Minion costumes. Consequently, Kit, as spokesperson for this network, influences the others to surrender their private judgement. We recognise that this chapter focuses on Amy's hypothetical story of how having a policy will enact authority, rather than the actual doing of authority. Nevertheless, the analyses do show Amy's orientation to how she imagines authority will be played out by invoking policy. The reconstructed dialogue that Amy uses mirrors the way in which Benoit-Barné and Cooren (2009) demonstrate the actual doing of authority in interaction. In their analysis of naturally occurring interaction, Benoit-Barné and Cooren (2009) show how a medical coordinator of Médecins sans Frontières ventriloquises a memo as part of in situ workplace practice and so "does" authority. Second, we note that Kit and Amy both ventriloquise networks of actants, attributing agency to them and mobilising them to account for their actions. To paraphrase Cooren (2016: 19), since rendering oneself accountable is a fundamental character of "human" interaction, we should take seriously who or what human interactants claim caused them to say what they say or do what they do. This, of course, brings us back to Latour's (1996) observation that "to do is causing to do", which scholars from the Montreal School would argue needs to be taken into account if a fully nuanced analysis of the communicative constitution of the organisation is to be had, as demonstrated in this chapter. Indeed, because ventriloquial analyses provide an excellent way of scaling up from discourse (talk in interaction) to phenomena of interest to organisation scholars (such as authority), they are becoming an increasingly popular way of investigating the communicative constitution of organisations. We think that it is certainly worth considering whether your own particular research interests can be advanced by using a ventriloquial lens.

Observations for Practice and Conclusions

The growing interest in materiality and ventriloquism within organisational studies not only offers new perspectives for researchers but also presents valuable insights for management practice and consultancy work. Ventriloquism research can help consultants by guiding their attention to interactional episodes that facilitate the systematic inquiry into organising and organisation. By understanding how people ventriloquise other actants—policies, missions, facts, persons, etc.—that can then be deemed to be participating in or influencing an interaction, the consultant can gain insights into power dynamics, key influencers, and areas for improved communication and collaboration.

Now that our ears are honed to notice the practice of ventriloquising, we can have a look at the following informal interaction between Amy and Dot through the eyes of a consultant. The discussion was recorded as they were walking towards the room that Dot was supposed to set up for an important meeting with upper management.

Extract 8.3

1	Dot:	what's the process (0.5) I want to use a seminar room and I need to use the IT
2		and stuff in there who = who do I actually speak to that isn't Rick↑
3	Amy:	do you think there's a process do you↑[((laughs))
4	Dot:	[((laughs))
	(14 lines omitted)	
18	Amy:	okay euh I would speak to Tom (.) because he has done that
19	Dot:	okay

20	Amy:	before the board [meeting
21	Dot:	[okay
22	Amy:	and just ask him if there's a process
23	Dot:	okay
24	Amy:	but usually Rick is the process right now which I'm not saying it's right but
25	Dot:	yeah
26	Amy:	that is what's happening

In line 1, Dot asks "what's the process" if she wants to use a seminar room and the IT equipment. She thus invokes the idea that a written, or unwritten, process should lead her to act in a certain way—the process matters to her. Amy treats this ironically by asking if Dot thinks there is a process and then laughing as she completes her utterance. Dot aligns with this irony by laughing with Amy, thus treating the lack of a process as something that is laughable. We then omit 14 lines, after which the talk returns to the question of how to book the rooms and IT equipment. In lines 18–24, Amy suggests that Dot should ask Tom if there is a process despite the fact that "Rick is the process right now". She assesses this situation equivocally: "I'm not saying it's right but that is what's happening".

In ventriloquial terms, not having a process that, on the one hand, can animate organisational players and tell them what to do and, on the other hand, can be animated by organisational players to account for what they do (as seen in Extracts 8.1 and 8.2) is treated as a laughable situation. Being able to ventriloquise a process (or a protocol, as in Extracts 8.1 and 8.2) is a way of scaling up from the local interaction to the organisation as made present in, and through, a process that is transportable over space and time and made relevant in an interaction. The fact that in Extract 8.1, there is no process, or at least not an acceptable one, means that the organisation, writ large, cannot be made present and in some way fails or is treated as laughable. This realisation of the practical importance of the way in which organisation relies on ventriloquising other-than-human processes and protocols is interesting for anyone—researcher or practitioner—involved in analysing organising and organisations.

Knowing the history of the organisational changes, the relative youth of the team, and previous tensions between upper management and the fundraising team, the observations we can make about Extracts 8.1–8.3 are not surprising considering the ways in which problems related to authority and the lack of a protocol (Extracts 8.1 and 8.2) and a process (Extract 8.3) could adversely affect the functioning of the fundraising team. Here, we have shown how a ventriloquial lens can expose and bring to the level of consciousness organisational issues—such as a lack of processes or policies—that arguably have a strong effect on the functioning of the team. In the next chapter, we will explore whether, and how, these issues can be remedied—if at all.

References

Bencherki, N. (2014). L'ethnométhodologie et l'École de Montréal (Ethnomethodology and The Montreal School). In H. Bourdeloire & Douyère (Eds.) *Méthodes de recherche sur l'information et la communication* (Information and Communication Research Methods) (pp. 141–166).

Bencherki, N. (2016). How things make things do things with words, or how to pay attention to what things have to say. *Communication Research and Practice, 2*(3), 272–289.

Benoit-Barné, C., & Cooren, F. (2009). The accomplishment of authority through presentification: How authority is distributed among and negotiated by organizational members. *Management Communication Quarterly, 23*(1), 5–31.

Bourgoin, A., & Bencherki, N. (2013). *The performance of authority in organizations: An example from management consulting* (Centre de Sociologie de l'Innovation Working Paper N°29). http://www.csi.mines-paristech.fr/workingpapers/DLWP.php?wp=WP_CSI_029.pdf

Callon, M. (1986). The sociology of an actor-network. In M. Callon, J. Law, & A. Rip (Eds.), *Mapping the dynamics of science and technology* (pp. 19–34). Macmillan.

Carlile, P., Nicolini, D., Langley, A., & Tsoukas, H. (2013). Introducing the third volume of perspectives on organisational studies. In P. Carlile, D. Nicolini, A. Langley, & H. Tsoukas (Eds.), *How matter matters* (pp. 1–16). Oxford University Press.

Caronia, L., & Cooren, F. (2014). Decentering our analytical position: The dialogicity of things. *Discourse & Communication, 8*(1), 41–61.

Castor, T., & Cooren, F. (2006). Organizations as hybrid forms of life: The implications of the selection of agency in problem formulation. *Management Communication Quarterly, 19*(4), 57.

Clifton, J., & de La Broise, P. (2020). The yellow vests and the communicative constitution of a protest movement. *Discourse & Communication, 14*(4), 362–382.

Cooren, F. (2001). Translation and articulation in the organization of coalitions: The Great Whale River case. *Communication Theory, 11*(2), 178–200.

Cooren, F. (2010). *Action and agency in dialogue: Passion, incarnation, and ventriloquism*. John Benjamins.

Cooren, F. (2012). Communication theory at the center: Ventriloquism and the communicative constitution of reality. *Journal of Communication, 62*, 1–20.

Cooren, F. (2015). Studying agency from a ventriloquial perspective. *Management Communication Quarterly, 29*(3), 475–480.

Cooren, F. (2016). Ethics for dummies: Ventriloquism and responsibility. *Atlantic Journal of Communication, 24*(1), 17–30.

Cooren, F., & Matté, F. (2010). For a constitutive pragmatics: Obama, Médecins Sans Frontières and the measuring stick. *Pragmatics and Society, 1*(1), 9–31.

Cooren, F., Fairhurst, G., & Huët, R. (2012). Why matter always matters in (organizational) communication. In P. Leonardi, B. Nardi, & J. Kallinikos (Eds.), *Materiality and organizing: Social interaction in a technological world* (pp. 296–314). Oxford University Press.

Cooren, F., Kuhn, T., Cornelissen, J. P., & Clark, T. (2011). Communication, organizing and organization: An overview and introduction to the special issue. *Organization Studies, 32*(9), 1149–1170.

Fairhurst, G. T., & Cooren, F. (2009). Leadership as the hybrid production of presence(s). *Leadership, 5*(4), 469–490.

Garfinkel, H. (1967). *Studies in ethnomethodology*. Prentice-Hall.

Goffman, E. (1981). *Forms of talk*. University of Pennsylvania Press.

Latour, B. (1996). On interobjectivity. *Mind, Culture, and Activity, 3*(4), 228–245.

Latour, B. (2005). *Reassembling the social: An introduction to actor-network theory*. Oxford University Press.

Latour, B. (2010). Forward. In F. Cooren (Ed.), *Action and agency in dialogue: Passion, incarnation and ventriloquism*, (pp. xiii–xvi). John Benjamins.

Law, J. (1992). Notes on the theory of the actor-network: Ordering, strategy, and heterogeneity. *Systems Practice, 5*(4), 379–393.

McPhee, R., & Iveson, J. (2013). Activity coordination and the Montreal School. In D. Robichaud & F. Cooren (Eds.), *Organization and organizing. Materiality, agency and discourse* (pp. 109–124). Routledge.

Nathues, E., Vuuren, M. V., & Cooren, F. (2021). Speaking about vision, talking in the name of so much more: A methodological framework for ventriloquial analyses in organization studies. *Organization Studies, 42*(9), 1457–1476.

Shaw, C., Hepburn, A., & Potter, J. (2013b). Having the last laugh: On post-completion laughter particles. In P. Glenn & E. Holt (Eds), *Studies of laughter in interaction* (pp. 91–106). Bloomsbury.

Tannen, D. (1989). *Talking voices: Repetition, dialogue, and imagery in conversational discourse*. Cambridge University Press.

Weber, M. (1978). *Economy and society*. University of California Press.
Wilhoit, E. D., & Kisselburgh, L. G. (2019). The relational ontology of resistance: Hybridity, ventriloquism, and materiality in the production of bike commuting as resistance. *Organization, 26*(6), 873–893.

CHAPTER 9

Concluding the Case: A Road to Organisational Healing

Introduction

If you have started this book by taking a sneak peek at the last chapter to find out how the story ends, the word "healing" may not be the closure you were hoping for. Indeed, while the story of our consultancy and the case study ends here, the real story for the income generation team only begins. We came across the notion of healing while chatting to Dot. In her interview, she explained to us about the "hurt" that surfaced during her management training and that the "healing process" started with the hiring of Amy and the new team.

Extract 9.1

1	Dot:	I think (.) as a hospice is ahome (0.6) euh as a home (.) that's telling isn't it↑
2		erm think yes(.) that it came out in this whole middle management erm course
3		that we did (.) it t was all very positive, very posi-until we started to talk about
4		the past in the last day (.) and then the whole atmosphere <u>changed</u> so e::r
5		there's a lot of=in the hospices itself (.) there's a lot of hurt still er an=and not
6		about what was done but how everything was done and (1) er but we have
7		different management now (.) the people that were involved in that

E. Darics and J. Clifton, *Organisation, Communication and Language*, New Perspectives in Organizational Communication,
https://doi.org/10.1007/978-3-031-30199-5_9

8 have mainly moved on (.) we have new trustees er so the healing process
9 is there within our team (.) I think (.) because we are so new we're very much
10 looking forward and trying to build on what we've got and and make it not
11 necessarily bigger just better

Perhaps it is not surprising that Dot spoke about hurt and healing, considering the context in which the consultancy took place. After all, the primary goal of any hospice is to improve the quality of life for patients and their families during the end-of-life process, manage the pain and other symptoms, and provide emotional and spiritual support. We mentioned in Chapter 3 that physical settings can act as triggers for metaphors (Kövecses, 2010), and, arguably, that is the case in Dot's example when she talks about the outcome of the organisational change in terms of a healing process. Whatever the inspiration, though, organisational healing seems to be an apt metaphor to contextualise the fundraising team's past experience and help to define future actions to re-dynamise the team.

This chapter is structured as follows. First, we introduce why linguistic-discourse analytic approaches to organisational text and talk are well-suited to reveal issues that may have led to a situation that requires healing and remedy. We take stock of the approaches we covered in the book and use an example to demonstrate how these methods can be applied to the same data so as to bring to the level of consciousness details that otherwise may have gone unnoticed. Then we turn our attention to the healing process itself, both generally and for our fundraising team. We conclude the chapter with takeaway points for research and practice.

The Need for Organisational Healing: Causes, Symptoms, and Language

Organisational healing is based on the idea that organisations, like people, can experience trauma, dysfunction, and other negative states that can hinder their ability to function effectively (Powley & Cameron, 2006). These issues can arise from various root causes, such as restructuring, leadership problems, or external factors such as the introduction of a new funding system (as in the case of our fundraising team), or indeed a global pandemic (e.g. Stranzl et al., 2021). And just as with people, unprocessed trauma or hurt within an organisation can have severe and long-lasting consequences, leading to a perpetuating cycle of negativity that can erode trust, damage employee morale, and undermine overall organisational effectiveness (Powley, 2011; Venugopal, 2016). Traumatic effects can be made worse if organisations do not communicate in a transparent way. Lack of transparency, as Stranzl et al. (2021: 273) found, "may enhance employees' uncertainty and anxiety experienced during times of crisis and cause them to disengage from their job by disconnecting from their work roles". The cycle of negative experiences and the resulting symptoms can manifest themselves in various forms, both at individual and team level. It goes without saying that in order to turn an organisation around from a downward spiral that could potentially even lead to its demise (Venugopal, 2016), it is crucial to recognise the dangers of unprocessed trauma. Ending this downward spiral, as business consultants attest (e.g. Knight, 2015), is often easier said than done for two reasons: on the one hand, trauma may not be immediately apparent and, on the other hand, it may reveal itself in different ways. Close attention to detail in communication, including micro-level analysis and a social constructionist approach to language and communication that we advocate in this book, offers a fruitful way to address both of these issues. Let us explore these in detail.

In terms of being apparent or not, experiences can be brought to the level of consciousness (for researchers and participants alike!) by paying close attention to how organisational members make sense of them during critical time periods (e.g. Powley, 2009). The focus on the sense-making process requires us to consider how meanings materialise—primarily through the minutiae and mechanics of language, talk, and communication. As Weick et al. (2005: 410) advocate, researchers and practitioners need to develop a greater appreciation for "smallness" because, as they put it, such "small structures and short moments can have large consequences". In this book, we advocated and demonstrated just how much we can learn by listening to, revealing, and understanding the significance of the details of ways of talking and writing.

- In Chapter 3, we showed the importance of noticing differences in conceptual thinking through the metaphors that team members use.
- In Chapter 4, we focused on language that team members use to categorise leaders and concluded how these team members influence leaders through linguistic category work.
- In Chapter 5, we analysed the stories team members tell to discover

how they resort to rumour to make sense of their uncertain organisational realities.
- In Chapter 6, we scrutinised the voice with which the organisation speaks to the outside world via Twitter, and demonstrated that the identity it projects is fragmented.
- In Chapter 7, we listened in on the team's conversations to discover how they use shared laughter and self-deprecating humour to "do" being a team.
- In Chapter 8, we turned our attention to how team members ventriloquise processes and policies and we revealed how the lack of processes and policies effects efficiency.

In terms of the different manifestations—or symptoms—of trauma, the extensive list of trauma symptoms in work organisations are well documented (see, for example, de Klerk, 2007). The list includes several symptoms we discussed throughout the book: anxiety, as we have seen through the emotionally charged language about the restructuring in Chapter 3; cynicism and diminished loyalty, as manifested in the critique of upper management in Chapter 4; uncertainty about the future and the emergence of rumour in Chapter 5; a fragmented sense of identity and, as a result, an incoherent organisational voice in Chapter 6; heightened emotions and the efforts to re-establish bonds between team members in Chapter 7; and issues related to authority and a lack of policies and processes that seem to adversely affect workflow in Chapter 8. The conceptual and analytical frameworks we introduced in the book (along with others such as positioning theory in Darics and Clifton (2019), or grounded theory in Powley, 2009) are very effective in revealing how the symptoms come to the surface, how organisational members talk their realities into being, or how they justify them. For example, in Chapter 7 we discuss "team spirit", a concept that is not easy to define and even harder to pin down. Team spirit, shared identity, and belonging are key guiding constructs if we want to understand and address organisational trauma, because in normal circumstances teams provide psychological safety. Team members trust and support each other, and the positive environment leads to better engagement and higher productivity (Stephens et al., 2011). Following a traumatic event, organisational members can become distrustful, their loyalty diminishes, and they may feel rejected and may withdraw (de Klerk, 2007), while at the same time they may feel a greater sense of belonging to a smaller group or look for deeper social connections with people they have not connected with before (Powley, 2009). Exploring and revealing how team members "do" team spirit, for example, through affiliative language (*we*), co-constructed turns, and shared laughter, makes visible how organisational members talk their reality of being a (new or functioning) team into being.

Diagnostic Listening

In an earlier study, we called the ability to notice and "to make visible, tangible, and thus actionable, the seen but unnoticed underlying assumptions, unshared information, and patterns of collective thinking" *diagnostic listening* (Darics & Clifton, 2019: 918). In this paper, we introduced one analytical approach—positioning theory—as a tool to conduct such diagnostic listening. In this book, we extend the diagnostic listening tool kit to metaphor analysis, membership categorisation analysis, narrative analysis and interactional sociolinguistics, metadiscourse analysis, conversation analysis, and ventriloquial analysis. Each of these methods shares a commonality: the primary focus of research is on the fine details of language and communication. Each method is based on the assumption that meaning and reality are socially constructed through language and communication. In terms of the analytical steps, each of these approaches is qualitative and interpretative, and requires the analyst to conduct micro-level, context-sensitive analyses of actual text and talk, examining the details of language use and communication at the level of individual words, phrases, or conversational turns. The difference between them is the analytical approach and theoretical orientation concerning the attention they pay to different aspects of social reality.

In the previous chapters, we introduced the approaches individually, provided a thorough conceptual background in relation to a specific organisational phenomenon, and demonstrated how the method can be used to theorise, and how it informs scholarship and possibly practice. Now, we invite you to try out your newly acquired knowledge and examine a short data extract through different analytical lenses. Academic researchers have previously tried this approach, whereby they applied different analytical approaches to analyse the same dataset. For example, Cooren (2013) brought together scholars from the fields of organisational communication and language and social interaction to analyse the same data, notably video recordings of a series of corporate management meetings drawn from a TV documentary, from different perspectives. Similarly,

Stubbe et al. (2003) analysed a nine-minute excerpt from a workplace meeting applying five different analytical approaches including conversation analysis and interactional sociolinguistics (these we also introduce in this book). These scholarly works demonstrate what different analytical approaches can reveal about the complex interplay between different linguistic forms and social context. In the following, we invite you to examine a much shorter excerpt—a genre which we have not addressed in the book thus far: a telephone message. In Extract 9.2 Amy calls a supplier to order T-shirts for an event. She cannot reach the supplier but leaves a message on his phone.

Extract 9.2

1	Amy:	((Phone rings)) hi umm (0.5) Ray it's Amy from Hospice (.) can you give me a
2		call↑ erm I'm actually gonna be in meetings quite a bit today (.) but erm
3		perhaps try my mobile ((gives number)) just to talk about how we get rou:::nd
4		either getting a hundred or a hundred and fifty t-shirts to us as soon as possible↑
5		while we sort the invoice out↓ erm we in = inherently have quite a slow
6		system here so::: I can't wait to order the t-shirts if you have to wait
7		to get paid for half the invoice if that makes sense (.) so can we see what
8		what we can do↓ if not we'll have to go to another supplier er so
9		erm ((Laughs)) so let me know (1) thanks Ray bye ((Hangs up phone))

Not all analytical frameworks are relevant or meaningful to apply to this text—there are no notable metaphors, for example. We can examine the text applying ***membership categorisation analysis*** (see Chapter 4). For example, we can identify membership categorisation devices which Amy uses to explicitly create category memberships: pronouns (I, we) and explicit descriptions (from the Hospice, another supplier) create category relations of hospice worker and (T-shirt) supplier. Next, we can look at what predicates are attributed to these categories: here, Amy describes her role as a worker at the hospice as well as a customer of Ray: "gonna be in meetings quite a bit today" and "we inherently have quite a slow system here" display her actions and constraints as an organisational member; and "can't wait to order the t-shirts" and "have to go to another supplier" show her expectations or possible actions as a customer. What is interesting here is the action that the category work achieves. First, while the categories of "supplier" and "hospice worker" are, in theory, interdependent roles (Amy needs the service, while Ray needs custom/payment), Amy's language reveals a different category relation: that of power and authority. While carefully encoded in obscure grammar ("I can't wait to order the t-shirts if you have to wait to get paid for half the invoice") and the use of the politeness strategy to mitigate the request ("if that makes sense" and laughter at the end of her turn), Amy is essentially negotiating a delay in payments by giving an ultimatum to the supplier: "or we will have to go to another supplier". We can see that membership categorisation analysis (membership categorisation devices, predicates, and category relations) allow us to expose both the conceptualisation of Amy of herself as an organisational member and the unequal power relations between the hospice and its suppliers.

To examine the linguistic and discourse strategies, she uses to negotiate the relationship between herself, the organisation she represents, and the supplier, we can use *interactional sociolinguistics* (as we introduced in Chapter 5). Interactional sociolinguistics guides our attention to contextualisation cues that Amy uses to help Ray interpret her messages. For example, her regular hesitations serve as cues that contextualise content that may not be perceived favourably. We see this first when she asks Ray to call her back because she is in meetings all day, and then when she explains the problems with payments. Here, hesitations contextualise her messages to signal that she is perhaps uncomfortable with the directness of the message, especially the implicit threat to go to another supplier if Ray is not prepared to wait for the payment (see the long hesitation in line 9). The laughter in line 9 serves a similar purpose of mitigating the imposition of the threat, thus trying to create a more respectful, polite atmosphere.

Finally, we can explore this extract to gain a better understanding of the organisational identity that is made visible through Amy's language use. As we explained in Chapter 6, organisational identity is crucial for the successful functioning of an organisation and is projected from within the organisation towards external stakeholders. Here, we can combine insights from metadiscourse analysis with insights from ventriloquial analysis. Looking at the pronouns Amy uses, she obviously distinguishes between herself as speaker and Ray the supplier through the use of singular first person and second person pronouns. The use of the plural first person pronoun "we" is interesting, however, because she uses it in an inclusive way to mean those present in the interaction, i.e. Ray and herself (line 3: "how we get round"), as well as in an exclusive manner to refer to herself and the organisation she represents: in line 5, "while we sort the invoice out", or in line 8, "we'll have to go to another supplier". This shift in meaning enables Amy to oscillate between personal and corporate voice, notably when she communicates the unfavourable messages of delayed payment and the condition of the delay. Viewing this message through the lens of ventriloquism allows us to notice the authoritative identity of the organisation she makes relevant: she animates the "system", which is inherently slow to legitimise the payment. The authority of the organisation is also mobilised through her sentence in lines 7–8: "so can we see what what we can do↓ if not we'll have to go to another supplier er so erm ((Laughs)) so let me know". This allows her to downplay her own agency in the decision to look for another supplier. This subtle ventriloquism has the effect of threatening Ray without being too direct or aggressive. As we have noticed above, she also laughs and says "er so erm" to mitigate the threat and show some hesitation or embarrassment.

Through the analysis of Amy's phone message, we have showcased how different approaches can be combined to gain a comprehensive understanding of the text, revealing the conceptualisation of Amy as an organisational member, her negotiation of power relations with the supplier, the linguistic and discourse strategies she employs to mitigate the imposition of her request, and the organisational identity projected through her language use. We hope that this holistic analysis has proved the usefulness of what we called diagnostic listening, as it can make visible, tangible, and actionable the seen but unnoticed aspects of organisational life, including areas requiring intervention or improvement.

On the Path of Organisational Healing

Powley (2011: 857) defines organisational healing "as a process of positive, enabling social interactions to restore and renew organisation members' interpersonal connections and allow the organisation to resume routines, practices, or operations". The uniqueness of this definition lies in its difference from more traditional concepts such as resilience, hardiness, and recovery (Vogus & Sutcliffe, 2007) because it highlights the actual work of repairing and mending the collective social fabric of an organisation after a crisis. As Powley (2013) notes, healing, more than resilience, coping, or recovery, enables greater organisational strength than what previously existed because it focuses on the work of repairing practices, routines, and structures and strengthening organisational functioning through social relationships. This process is inherently social and constructed through interactions among organisational members. By adopting a social constructionist lens, as we have proposed in this book, it is possible to explore the ways in which language and communication practices contribute to the process of healing, whether through talking new practices, routines and structures into being or through establishing new social relationships.

Extending the metaphor of healing further by observing physiological healing, Powley (2013) distinguishes three stages of healing. Stage 1 (which he compares to protective inflammation) is the immediate focused response to a crisis or traumatic event. In organisational contexts, this is the critical first reaction stage that aims to stabilise the situation and ensure the well-being of the organisational members. That is, of course, if key organisational players realise that a crisis is happening. However, as we demonstrated in Chapter 5, the events unfolding at the hospice suggest that key organisational players may not have realised the existence of crisis. Instead, rumours emerged, and without clear communication, organisational members had to make sense of their reality based on the available information. In contrast to the physiological response of the body when hurt, the healing process at the hospice could not start until key players recognised the existence of the undiscovered and unprocessed trauma.

During the next phase of healing in the human body, known as "proliferation" in physiology, the focus shifts to repairing the damage by replacing it with healthy tissue. Understood metaphorically, the proliferation phase directs our attention to the strengthening of new external and internal networks of relationships. In a managed healing process, this stage focuses on building positive relationships "to reenergize and inspire commitment in units with low morale" (Powley, 2013: 49). Interactions are key in this stage, as individuals create new relationships, develop trust, and share stories and emotions. In our case study, we observed several examples of such interactions, but they occurred in an uncontrolled, bottom-up manner. For instance, during the interviews, core team members sought validation for their thoughts and feelings by sharing their traumatic experiences with us, consultants (see Chapters 2 and 3). In another context team members and the new head of income generation, Amy, created an antagonist split between upper management and team members (Chapter 4). We have also observed how different interpretations of the situation arose through storytelling (Chapter 5).

The final stage of healing is the return to full functionality, but with a structure that is stronger and more resilient than the previous one. In his study, Powley (2013) uses the case of the housing market crash in 2008 and demonstrates how people in a financial institution restructure their practices and routines through learning from their mistakes and successes and how their new practice had greater strength and resilience than before. This is a bottom-up process where a new organisational identity, practices, routines, and social relationships are co-constructed by all involved, because as Mills et al. (2005: 614) noted, "they cannot be formulated by a leader and simply bestowed upon the members … [they] must emerge from the interactions of those involved in the organization". In the hospice we, together with our readers, were privileged to witness the beginning of this process. As Dot's words in Extract 9.1 show, the members of the fundraising team were ready and looking "forward and trying to build on what they've got and make it not necessarily bigger just better". The team made concrete steps to achieve this—as a start, they invited consultants in the hope of making the healing process happen. Throughout the book, we have shown aspects of organisational realities we encountered during this consultancy and shared with you the findings. Based on these findings, we recommended courses of action for the fundraising team and the larger organisation. How successful these will be only time will tell. But this book will remain as a record of the transformative power of language and communication. We hope it will also serve as a gentle reminder to all organisational members: when crisis strikes, remember to listen, learn, and rebuild together. It is in this collective endeavour that we find not just healing but empowerment and growth.

Final Takeaway

For Researchers

In this book, we have advocated and demonstrated research approaches that pay meticulous attention not just to the small details in language and communication but also to their closer and broader linguistic and discourse contexts, while remaining deeply embedded in wider social realities. By embracing the dialectical relationship between language and social context, we have demonstrated the power of a comprehensive approach to the study of language and communication in the workplace.

Such an approach is much needed because, as Gummesson (2017: 145) reminds us, research often consists of fragments that, while interesting in themselves, make little sense without being tied together into a context. This book showcased how to bridge that gap. On the one hand, we invited organisational scholars to engage with empirical language data and draw on findings, methods, and theories from language-focused discourse studies, and, on the other hand, we invited linguists and discourse analysts to consider the broader practical and theoretical implications of their scholarly work in the context of organisations, organising, and work processes.

In a world where interactions and verbal, textual, and visual data pervade our working and personal lives, it can be impossible to pay attention to everything. However, when issues arise, the discourse and linguistic theories and analytical methods advocated in this book can serve as both a magnifying glass to uncover hidden issues and can function as a map to connect the dots and identify patterns and themes across text, interactions, and events. The ability to find patterns in a mass of data is a truly valuable skill that will enable you to "maintain an open mind and synthesise diverse data into a cohesive whole" (Gummesson, 2017: 55).

Our knowledge that enables us to reveal how ways of talking and writing can create versions of reality naturally pushes us to ask questions about the type of reality that is being created. Organisations, organising, leadership, and management are never neutral and, as Grey (2004: 179) aptly puts it, "To engage in management, or to research management, is to commit to some stance on political and moral values, such as the desirability of efficiency, or of productivity, or of profitability, or even of employee satisfaction and well-being". A social constructionist lens requires the researcher to reflect and bring to the level of consciousness these stances: the terra firma of real-life empirical data will, inevitably, bring to the surface the ideologies and power relations, practices, routines, and interests that influence the production of text and talk. Such critical observations can help you go beyond mere description to challenge problematic power structures, ideologies, and underlying values.

For Practice

Addressing Gummesson's (2017: 146) critique on the gap between theory and action in business and management, this book bridges that gap by highlighting the transformative potential of linguistic-discourse analytic approaches in bringing about tangible change within organisations. We join other colleagues who advocate this approach. Baxter (2017), for example, gives an excellent example of the usefulness of discourse analysis for consultancy research that aims to solve communication problems within organisations. In her study, Baxter (2017: 156) promotes the use of transcripts of significant moments as a "feedback method that could also be deployed with whole teams". By showing a team how small moments of interaction within meetings can construct organisational practices, such collaborative analysis can prompt peer discussions and the collective realisation of previously unnoticed practices. During such collaborations, knowledge is co-created and, as Camargo-Borges and Rasera (2013: 5) argue, "it is not taken as only a description of something that happened, but it constructs change within the organisation, and its members are the immediate beneficiaries of it".

In conclusion, we want to highlight the transformative potential of being aware of one's own language use for researchers, practitioners, and managers. By delving into linguistic-discourse analytic approaches, we become sensitised to the process of how language constructs our social realities. Inns (2002: 326) emphasises that this awareness serves as a tool that goes beyond merely appropriating organisational sense-giving, and instead, it leads to genuine empowerment for organisational members. With this in mind, we encourage you to embrace the power of language and communication as a means to not only foster positive change through your research or within your organisation but also to empower yourself and others along the way.

References

Baxter, J. (2017). Resolving a gender and language problem in women's leadership: Consultancy research in workplace discourse. *Discourse & Communication, 11*(2), 141–159.

Camargo-Borges, C., & Rasera, E. F. (2013). Social constructionism in the context of organization development: Dialogue, imagination, and co-creation as resources of change. *Sage Open*, *3*(2).

Cooren, F. (Ed.). (2013). *Interacting and organizing: Analyses of a management meeting*. Routledge.

Darics, E., & Clifton, J. (2019). Making applied linguistics applicable to business practice. Discourse analysis as a management tool. *Applied Linguistics, 40*(6), 917–936.

de Klerk, M. (2007). Healing emotional trauma in organizations: An OD framework and case study. *Organization Development Journal, 25*(1), 49–55.

Grey, C. (2004). Reinventing business schools: The contribution of critical management education. *Academy of Management Learning & Education, 3*(2), 178–186.

Gummesson, E. (2017). *Case theory in business and management: Reinventing case study research*. Sage.

Inns, D. (2002). Metaphor in the literature of organizational analysis: A preliminary taxonomy and a glimpse at a humanities-based perspective. *Organization, 9*(2), 305–330.

Kövecses, Z. (2010). *Metaphor: A practical introduction*. Oxford university press.

Knight, R. (2015, October 14). What to do and say after a tough reorganization. *Harvard Business Review*. https://hbr.org/2015/10/what-to-do-and-say-after-a-tough-reorganization

Mills, M., Bettis, P., Miller, J. W., & Nolan, R. (2005). Experiences of academic unit reorganization: Organizational identity and identification in organizational change. *The Review of Higher Education, 28*(4), 597–619.

Powley, E. H. (2009). Reclaiming resilience and safety: Resilience activation in the critical period of crisis. *Human Relations, 62*(9), 1289–1326.

Powley, E. H. (2011). Organizational healing: A relational process to handle major disruption. In G. Spreitzer & K. Camero (Eds.), *The Oxford handbook of positive organizational scholarship* (pp. 856–866). Oxford University Press.

Powley, E. H. (2013). The process and mechanisms of organizational healing. *The Journal of Applied Behavioral Science, 49*(1), 42–68. https://doi.org/10.1177/0021886312471192

Powley, E. H., & Cameron, K. S. (2006). Organizational healing: Lived virtuousness amidst organizational crisis. *Journal of Management, Spirituality & Religion, 3*(1–2), 13–33.

Stephens, J. P., Heaphy, E., & Dutton, J. E. (2011). High-quality connections. In G. Spreitzer & K. Cameron (Eds.), *The Oxford handbook of positive organizational scholarship* (pp. 385–399). Oxford University Press.

Stranzl, J., Ruppel, C., & Einwiller, S. (2021). Examining the role of transparent organizational communication for employees' job engagement and disengagement during the COVID-19 pandemic in Austria. *Journal of International Crisis and Risk Communication Research, 4*(2), 271–308.

Stubbe, M., Lane, C., Hilder, J., Vine, E., Vine, B., Marra, M., & Weatherall, A. (2003). Multiple discourse analyses of a workplace interaction. *Discourse Studies, 5*(3), 351–388.

Venugopal, V. (2016). Understanding organizational trauma: A background review of types and causes. *Journal of Business and Management, 18*(10), 65–69.

Vogus, T. J., & Sutcliffe, K. M. (2007, October). Organizational resilience: Towards a theory and research agenda. In *2007 IEEE international conference on systems, man and cybernetics* (pp. 3418–3422). IEEE.

Weick, K. E., Sutcliffe, K. M., & Obstfeld, D. (2005). Organizing and the process of sensemaking. *Organization science, 16*(4), 409–421.

Appendix

List of Transcription Symbols Used

description of actions	((sighs))
word spoken with rising intonation	frightening↑
word spoken with falling intonation	Funky ↓
overlapping talk	[but
word spoken more softly than surrounding talk	make
word spoken more loudly than surrounding talk	OKAY
word spoken with emphasis	children
stretching of vowel sound	no::::
words latched	was = they
slight pause	(.)
pause in tenths of a second	(.7)
untranscribable word	()
word spoken with a "smile" voice	£ye::s£

E. Darics and J. Clifton, *Organisation, Communication and Language*, New Perspectives in Organizational Communication,
https://doi.org/10.1007/978-3-031-30199-5

Index

E. Darics and J. Clifton, *Organisation, Communication and Language*, New Perspectives in Organizational Communication,
https://doi.org/10.1007/978-3-031-30199-5

FSC
www.fsc.org
MIX
Papier | Fördert gute Waldnutzung
FSC® C083411

Kolibri 360 GmbH
Ferdinand-Jühlke-Straße 7
99095 Erfurt, Deutschland
produktsicherheit@kolibri360.de